College Poor No More

100 $avings Tips
for College Students

College Poor No More
100 Savings Tips for College Students
Copyright © 2019 by Michelle Perry Higgins

Additional copies may be ordered from the publisher
for educational, business,promotional or premium use.
For information, contact ALIVE Book Publishing at:
alivebookpublishing.com, or call (925) 837-7303.

ISBN 13
978-1-63132-074-3

ISBN 10
1-63132-074-2

Library of Congress Control Number: 2019910294
Library of Congress Cataloging-in-Publication Data
is available upon request.

Second Edition

Published in the United States of America by ALIVE Book Publishing
and ALIVE Publishing Group, imprints of Advanced Publishing LLC
3200 A Danville Blvd., Suite 204, Alamo, California 94507
alivebookpublishing.com

PRINTED IN THE UNITED STATES OF AMERICA

College Poor No More

100 $avings Tips
for College Students

Michelle Perry Higgins

MichellePerryHiggins.com

To Mom, my friend and mentor

CONTENTS

Hitting the Shops

Cooking, Eating, and Drinking

Social Life

81

Day-to-Day Living

95

Housing 113

Travel 123

Life Hacks 129

Professional Matters 139

Welcome to the Real World

Welcome
to College

Congratulations!

You've finally escaped high school and you're heading into some of the best, crazy-good years of your life. New friends, new experiences, new independence, and an incred- ible social scene eagerly await you. Your life will be forever changed the moment you walk into college. The next few years will start to define who you are as a person and pave the way toward a bright future.

So ... Welcome to college!

That phrase will describe anything and everything that happens while you're in college; all those crazy and exciting and sometimes surreal things that don't happen in normal society.

Are you eating Top Ramen and three Hot Pockets every day for a week because you can't afford real food?

Welcome to college.

Are you digging through your laundry for the shirt that looks and smells the cleanest because why pay $10 to clean your clothes, when cologne is just as good?

Welcome to college.

Have you stopped shaving because why spend money on a new razor, when you can tell your friends you're making *No-Shave November* a thing?

Welcome to college.

Is the amount of quarters you need to do your laundry equal in weight to your organic chemistry textbook?

Welcome to college.

Are you trusting your shaky-handed, sleep-deprived roommate to cut or dye your hair because $200 is way too much to spend on a haircut?

Welcome to college.

These are all things that you, or someone you know, might experience while away at school. If that frightens you, take a deep breath. This book offers heaps of tips to avoid the money shortages that plague most students and teach you how to get the most out of the dollars you have, which may just help you avoid the stomachache from a semester's worth of Hot Pockets, or the missing chunk in your hair from the slip of a roommate's scissors.

Are you reading this book at school, or perhaps before you head off?

Whether freshman year or senior year, there's always a sense of euphoria when you first arrive on campus. Your wal- let is full, your hair is precision-cut, your clothes are stylin', you're in Olympian-shape … you've got whatever it is that makes you feel good about yourself.

If it's your freshman year, you're excited to be finally free and on your own. If it's your sophomore year, you're happy to be finally out of the dorms. If it's your junior year, you're happy because you finally figured out the configuration of your school (and you may be turning 21). And if it's your senior year, you're ecstatic to graduate and start making some real cash.

No matter what year you're in, there isn't a single person who's not excited to be back on campus.

Those first few weeks are golden. Your checking account is full, your credit card has zero balance, and all your friends are in the same boat, sharing the wealth and all the fun that comes with it.

Whenever I returned to campus after summer break, I'd immediately call my girlfriends. We'd all go out to dinner and laugh and talk about our summers. We'd head to the mall that first Saturday on campus and they would run up their credit cards.

My friends would party with no worries in the world, like trust-fund babies. Too bad, so sad, that jubilation always came screeching to a halt in month two. Then, reality hit like the proverbial freight train when the bills showed up and they realized paying them would really deplete their checking accounts … and then some.

Nothing throws a college student into a terror tailspin faster than an empty bank account and a heap of unpaid bills, especially when Mom and Dad are not as generous that second month and won't extend you a single $20. Why not learn to head that unpleasant reality off at the pass? If there's no one but you to pay off that credit card bill, you'll need to figure out your finances pretty quick or your carefree college fun is over. Luckily, it's not that hard to do.

Here's the first thing you have to accept: you are poor. The good news? Being poor in college is neither a bad thing nor a rare thing. Most everyone around you will be poor as well. So, why not embrace poverty, college-style, for the creative challenge it is?

College is the transition stage between teenage/parent dependence and adult independence. Believe it or not, now is the time to learn money management skills. Now is the time to learn how to "just say no" to excesses you don't need, you can't afford, and if you're really honest, you might not even want all that badly.

But hey, living frugally doesn't mean having no fun. On the

contrary! It means finding creative and unique and sometimes crazy, out-of-the-box ways to get the most fun out of the least amount of money.

The 100 tips in this book are not complicated. Some are serious. Some are tongue-in-cheek. Some might be worth their weight in tuition gold.

I bet that after you read this book, you'll feel empowered to tackle your finances with a whole new outlook. I can't lie, though. It will take discipline *every day* to stay on a budget and manage your finances effectively.

Our goal? To minimize the amount of debt you'll graduate with and help you learn the value of money.

Are you up for the challenge? If so, good luck and …

Welcome to college!

Managing Your Money

The Right Financial Attitude Makes All the Difference

M anaging your money effectively is a fantastic skill, one I'm hoping to get you excited over. One I'm hoping you will take from this book. And one I'm hoping you will embrace and carry forward for the rest of your productive, successful, and fulfilling life. It all starts here.

Are you with me? Being in college might be your first experience of independence and handling your own finances. Why not learn to manage your money like a pro now? Why not learn to save it, grow it, and grow your self-respect, maturity, and confidence at the same time?

Let's do this! Ready to get financially fit and face all these new #moneyhacks head on?

Get Your College Allowance in Bite-Sized Chunks

When it comes to an allowance, getting monthly installments is like finances with training wheels. Perfect for learning how to handle your money.

Whether you're getting your living expenses from your parents, a scholarship, a loan, or a rich uncle, find out how to receive it in monthly installments instead of by semester, quarterly, or yearly. (With the exception of your tuition, of course.)

Getting a whole year's worth at once sounds like fun, doesn't it? That big check just screams freedom. But it might be a bit too much freedom. So think yearly, but act monthly. Remember my story about my first month at school each year and the wild spending sprees that went with it? Well, just picture yourself with a *full year's worth* of cash to burn. It's just human psychology; when we have a lot we feel free to spend a lot. It's all too easy to blow that money well before the semester is over and find yourself scrambling to pay bills and keep eating.

One of the best secrets to staying in a Ramen-free zone? Prioritizing. We'll talk more about that in future tips.

Budgets Are Sexy

E mbracing your poor-college-student status and learning to stick to a budget are signs of being a mature adult.

That's a good thing. It bodes well for your financial future.

Why not be as proud of being financially conscious as you are about being environmentally conscious, or politically conscious, or any other kind of conscious? Conscious is cool. Conscious is sexy.

Even when it comes to college dating, someone who can show you a good time without spending a fortune is pretty impressive, don't you think? Especially in today's expensive world. It requires creativity, imagination, and ingenuity—all sexy and attractive qualities.

Remember, most everyone in college lives on pennies. Saying, "I'm on a budget and unfortunately, that's not in it," is something most of your peers will understand and perhaps even admire.

Sure, spending money is hot. But what's even hotter is graduating college without unnecessary debt, debt that can drag behind you weighing you down for years after you graduate.

And who needs that? Not you.

CREATE A BUDGET SHEET

Now the financial fun really begins. Don't bail on me now. No matter how you receive your money—parents, student loans, or a job—it is essential to track your cash inflows and outflows so you're not stupefied or horrified at the end of the month—when your debit card is rejected.

Take this bull by its horns and go proactive. I recommend my clients keep a log, to know exactly how much they are receiving or earning, how much they are spending, and how much extra cash is left each month. You can use online programs like Mint.com or an Excel spreadsheet.

To get started:

- Decide which tracking method you want to use—on-line tools, Excel spreadsheet, apps.
- Make like a bloodhound and track every penny you spend for one month.
- Create categories that make sense to you.
- Create your budget in each category.

You'll probably find a convenient online app for your budget, but I've included an efficient, user-friendly sheet in Appendix A of this book, so you can get a sense of what I'm talking about.

Develop a structured bill-payment system as well, so you're never late for a payment. A site like Mint.com will send you reminders when a bill is due, or you can set them up yourself in your email calendar. This will keep your credit score high and your references in great shape.

FIGHT THE NEED TO BLOW EXTRA CASH

After a few months of analyzing your budget, you may find a little extra cash in your bank account. Woo-hoo!

You can think of a million things to spend it on – new jeans, a delicious meal, upgrading your phone, the list goes on. But I'm asking you to fight that urge. To go against every natural instinct. Instead of spending it … save it.

Surpluses leads to splurges. While a little splurge here or there is reasonable, don't feel the need to spend it *just because you can.*

Use your newfound budgeting skills for your rainy day fund, also known as an emergency reserve fund. This money will save your butt if you're ever in a pinch and need some extra cash. The chances you'll find yourself in that sort of a pinch are pretty high. Pinches happen to everyone, in college or out.

(Make sure you use any emergency reserves for an actual emergency and not a "desperate late-night Taco Bell" sort of situation.)

Think how great you'll feel when you do run into a situation requiring unexpected, unbudgeted-for money, and you have it! On your own, in your very own bank account, no parental save required.

SET UP A NO-FEE CHECKING ACCOUNT

Unless you're going to stuff your cash in your mattress (which I don't recommend), opening your own checking and savings account before you head off to college is crucial. Choose a bank with a branch on your college campus or close by.

#ParentHack: If possible, choose the same bank your parents use, so they can easily transfer funds to you or act as co-signers. Simply stated, you want to make it as easy as possible for them to give you money.

When choosing an account, the most important aspect is NO monthly fee. Five dollars a month may not seem like much at first, but that is $60 a year you are losing. That $60 could be a great end-of-year pizza party in the dorm instead. Better in your pocket than theirs!

Also, ask if the bank has student or college account options, or if they offer a rewards or cash-back program on educational purchases with your debit card.

Things to consider:

Is there an ATM fee or a withdrawal fee? Ask if they can be waived. You'd be surprised how much leeway the bank associate has to assist you.

Are there convenient bank and ATM locations near campus and home? If it's not convenient, it's not going to be worth it.

- If it's not where your parents bank, how can they transfer funds?
- Do either of your new accounts have a minimum balance requirement, and what happens if your balance goes below it? This one is crucial to know!
- Is there online banking and a mobile app?
- Do they offer text message alerts if your account goes below certain limits? (Also vital!)

Do It with Debit

Your trusty debit card gives you the ability to withdraw or deposit funds at the ATM and make purchases just about anywhere. One pitfall to be aware of: using a debit card is just like using cash. When you make a purchase, that amount is *immediately* deducted from your account. You must have the cash available.

If you look online for bank branches in your area, you'll know where to go in case you need some cash.

Another debit card pitfall: if you use the ATM from a different bank just because it's convenient, you'll be hit with a fee that will take your breath away, or should I say, take your carefully budgeted cash away. And there's nothing convenient about that.

SET UP AN ONLINE BANKING ACCOUNT

Once upon a time, in the pre-internet days, you got a monthly bank statement mailed to you. If you didn't keep good records in your checkbook throughout the month, it was easy to screw up your checking account. Too easy.

Now you can go paperless with online banking. You can check your balance on your laptop. You can check it on your phone. No wondering what is or isn't in your account. No wondering if your check is about to bounce, costing you a king's ransom in fees.

You never have to overdraw your account again. And that's a very good thing. All you need to set up online banking is a username and password. This gives you the ability to easily view, budget, manage, and wire funds online.

If you make it as easy as possible for your parents to give you money, they might just do it regularly. If they use the same bank, money transfers can be done with a couple of clicks.

Mobile apps make life even easier. Check your account balances 24/7 or even make a mobile deposit directly from your phone. If you're out and about and need to transfer money, or aren't sure if you have enough money, the app makes it super convenient.

IGNORE CREDIT CARD OFFERS
LIKE THE PLAGUE

Okay, that title is not exactly correct, because eventually you will want a credit card. You may even have one now under your parents' direction.

When you set up your new bank accounts, you'll be asked if you'd like a credit card. You'll receive dozens of credit card offers during the first few months of school as well. Just say no!

Before putting purchases on credit cards, why not first find out if you can make it on the money you have coming in? If you spend your first year of school developing strong budgeting skills, you might find you don't need or want a credit card.

If you do, perhaps wait until your junior year. By that time, most students understand how to live within their means.

Once you're ready for a credit card, let the hunt begin. You want a credit card with no annual fee, no hidden fees, and low interest rates. This last part is crucial, so please shop around. (The better your credit score, the lower the interest rates you'll qualify for, so all these financial tips really work together to save you money.)

Once you find the best credit card out of the hundreds available, I'd set up automatic monthly payments so you'll:

- Pay your bill *in full* each month.
- Pay your bill *on time.*

This prevents you from going into debt, and helps you build your credit score for the future.

Credit card companies love financially immature college students who fail to pay on time. They hit you with a late fee, and if you can't pay in full, they add on a huge interest charge.

But that's not going to be you. Don't let credit card debt ruin your college experience.

CHECK BALANCES WEEKLY

This is another tip that will help you sleep like a baby. Do you know how much you spent over the weekend? Or how much money is in your checking account and what your credit card bill is?

If you answered no to these questions, take a second and check. You may be surprised, shocked, or even horrified to find your balance is lower than you expected—way lower. This is information you need to know, for your own peace of mind and continued financial equanimity.

Sign-up for weekly *or even daily* emails containing your account balances. Get online and view your transactions. Here's why:

- Checking your balances and transactions keeps you more informed about your own finances, which is always a good thing.
- It allows you to track spending patterns and see where your money is really going. Starbucks? Pizza? Mani/pedis?
- It allows you to spot any unusual behavior in your accounts which could be identity theft or accounting errors made by your bank.
- You'll see right away if you are spending over budget and can course correct before you run into trouble.

CREDIT IS KING

People always say cash is king. I say *credit is king*. Having a good credit score might not be as much fun as scoring a date with your hot crush on campus, but it's definitely one of the most important financial attributes to possess. Credit is built on an ongoing basis, by your financial habits.

Pay your bills on time, don't let interest build up, and don't borrow what you cannot pay back. If you are on a well-thought-out budget and closely monitoring all your expenses, this will be a piece of cake.

Trust me, all your hard work will pay off. Buying your first home, that sexy sports car, or even getting into a posh apartment building in NYC right out of college will be a lot easier with a strong credit score. A poor credit score will make all of these purchases more expensive and sometimes impossible.

Some things that negatively impact your credit score include:
- Paying bills late
- Not paying the rent
- Not paying medical bills
- Canceling a gym membership improperly
- Ignored and unpaid traffic or parking tickets
- Not paying your bills to the point where they go to a collection agency

In the next tip, we'll talk more about why your credit score is worth paying attention to.

ONCE-A-YEAR CHECK-UP:
YOUR CREDIT REPORT

Since credit is king, give your credit score the attention and respect it deserves. After all, you have a credit score whether you know about it or not. Whether you check it or not. Whether you care about it or not.

So why not know what's going on? Information is power, right?

Your credit report tells banks and credit card companies and other agencies (like landlords and employers) how reli- able you are in paying your debts. The better your report, the higher your credit score.

The higher your credit score, the more likely an agency is to trust your money managing skills. This results in way better loan or mortgage or credit card rates. It can make the difference be- tween being able to afford something or not.

Under our current federal law, you are eligible for one *free* credit report every 12 months. You can receive it from each of the three major credit bureaus: TransUnion, Equifax, or Experian.

Credit reports can be erroneous if someone has stolen your identity or there's been some other kind of mix-up. Why not get in the habit of checking your credit report regularly?This will as- sure you that all the information on the report is correct and no identity theft has occurred.

Check your report at annualcreditreport.com (877) 322-8228

NEVER BORROW MORE
THAN YOU CAN PAY

I could never have gotten through college without student loans, and I'm forever grateful for them. But even with my positive experience, I still advise students to avoid student loans if at all possible. They rack up a huge amount of debt that you might be dragging behind you for years after you graduate.

The more you limit the amount of money you borrow, the less you'll have to pay back in the future. So, just because you qualify for a big loan does not mean you have to take all of it. The more accurately you've done your budget, the more clearly you'll know just how much of a loan you will need.

#PayItBackHack: If you do take a student loan, open a *separate savings account*. Don't commingle these funds with your day-to-day living expense money. It's just way too easy to blow through it. If you don't use those dollars during the school year, *pay back the loan immediately*.

EVALUATE YOUR OPPORTUNITY COSTS

I f you've taken any basic economics class, you know an *opportunity cost* is the cost of an alternative that must be forgone in order to pursue a certain action.

Say what?

In other words, what must you give up to do what you're currently doing? This is where we get into priorities. Everyone has them, and people who set them consciously can steer their lives more easily in the direction of what they want the most.

Life is full of opportunity costs and decisions you must make, especially now that there's no one forcing you to do anything.

For example, there's no one forcing you to get up in the mornings; therefore, you do not have to go to class. But sleeping in and not going to class is wasting the money that you have paid for that class, along with missing out on learning the material, receiving tips for tests, and getting the full benefit of the college education you're paying for.

I'd say the opportunity cost of sleeping in is too high.

Another way to think about opportunity costs is in terms of tradeoffs. If I spend money on X, then I will have less or maybe even no money to spend on Y.

Here's my classic example: "If I spend my money going out with friends (which I want to do), then I'll have less money to spend on groceries (and I really want to keep eating)."

These are the decisions you'll have to make on a daily basis. There is not necessarily a right and wrong answer, there are only choices—your choices, based on your priorities. So, set your priorities for your college experience overall. Choose wisely, think before you choose, and think twice before you spend.

Neither a Borrower nor a Lender Be

Avoid loaning money to your friends at all costs. Remember, you're all poor in college. It may take ages for your friend to pay you back. Are you willing to wait for years, until your best bud graduates and starts making the big bucks?

And what if he never pays you back at all?

Believe it or not, saying, "Sorry, I really can't spare the money right now," will be kinder on your friendship than loaning money and never seeing it again.

That said, situations do arise where loaning money or needing a loan is unavoidable. If that is the case, make a note on your phone about how much you owe your friend or your friend owes you.

As soon as you have the cash, pay your friend back. If you're the one making the loan, ask when your friend thinks he or she could pay it back. When that time comes, if your friend says nothing, it's perfectly acceptable to gently remind that person to pay you.

It is *not* impolite to ask. Straightforward financial dealings are a valuable skill you can learn now, before you need them in important business situations.

Don't ever be embarrassed to say, "I'm on a tight budget. I'd love to loan you the money, but I don't have it," or "I'm on a really tight budget and I'll need that money back by next Friday."

Check out money sharing apps such as Venmo or PayPal for instantaneous money transfers.

LIVE ON 90, SAVE 10

S pend less than you earn. Simple, right? Unfortunately, it's not so simple and a majority of Americans struggle with this.

But if you're one of the savvy ones who can spend less than you bring in, you're off to a fantastic financial start.

The importance of saving cannot be overstated. Saving can save your future. Even a few dollars a month can really add up. With the 90/10 rule, you can effectively and painlessly save fairly big bucks over the course of your college career and even more over your lifetime. No matter how much money you bring in, whether it's an allowance from your parents or income from your job, put 10% of it in savings.

Honest! Even saving $10 per month adds up to $120 in a year! Or $480 by the time you get your four-year degree. That's a pretty respectable nest egg for a previously penniless college student.

Perhaps you'll take that $480 and use it for a trip to New York City to interview for your dream job. Perhaps you'll use it as the security deposit on your fancy new post-college digs. Maybe spend it on plane fare for a much anticipated visit to your sweetheart across the country.

WARNING: Saving money, once you get the hang of it, can be highly addictive. Be careful or you might just wind up as a wealthy investor.

Keep your savings in a separate account from your check- ing account, so you don't wind up spending them without even thinking about it. To make it even easier, download mobile apps for automatic savings. Find out if your bank has one.

This strategy is a great way to begin saving for major events later in life, and it is both exciting and reassuring to see your savings rack up over time. And who doesn't like to see their money grow?

STOCKPILE CASH DURING THE SUMMER

Summer gives you the opportunity to make some real dough. What I'm about to recommend will be tough and go against every instinct, but try to save at least 50% (after taxes) of what you earn over the summer. Then you won't have to work as many hours during the school year, or perhaps not at all.

You'll feel rich when you get your first full-time, summer job paycheck. Enjoy the feeling. But as soon as that money starts burning a hole in your pocket, you'll want to hit the mall, go out to dinner, buy all your friends a round of drinks

… STOP!

Think back to the "ack!-I'm-a-poor-college-student" feeling you had last semester. The one you might just have again, as soon as you get back to school. And think how some—not all—but some of these summer paychecks might help relieve that feeling. With that thought in mind, immediately defer 50% (after taxes) of that impressive check into your emergency reserve savings account.

#CareerHack: Try to get a job in the field you're majoring in, to start getting your feet wet and build your resume. If you discover you don't enjoy that line of work (and many people have that experience), better to find out sooner than later, after you've spent four or more years learning it.

GET YOUR GROWNUP ON WITH A BROKERAGE OR RETIREMENT ACCOUNT

Yes, I said the "R" word: retirement. But why not start investing those extra pennies now? There mightnot be an abundance of extra cash in college, and there might be an overabundance of things to spend it on, but every little bit you invest now will make your future that much sweeter. If you are debt free and have extra cash above your emergency reserves and living expenses, consider investing this money.

I'm not talking about any funds you might need in the short term, because once it goes into the stock market, you need to view it as long-term investment (7+ years) that can weather stock market cycles. If you think you'll want to buy a home or a car with these funds in a few years (less than 7), do not put them into the stock market.

Explore different IRA (Individual Retirement Account) options and pick one that best fits your situation. Don't let that word "retirement" scare you or put you off. IRAs are a great way to save. It's the rare and unusual college student who would think so far ahead, and if you are that rare, savvy student, you can give yourself a high-five. You will be well ahead of the finance game in short order.

Not quite ready for the IRA route? Consider a brokerage account instead.

WARNING/DISCLAIMER: Do not pass "go" before taking the time to understand the pros & cons of each of these types of accounts. What are the restrictions, tax implications, costs, transaction fees, minimum investment, etc.?

#FinanceHack Plan of Attack: First, do your homework online to understand these different accounts. Consider this research just another part of your college education—a prac- tical and valuable part that can affect your future as much as anything else you are learning.

Second, turn to your parents and their financial planner or ac- countant for further guidance. I'm always available for my clients' kids. I want to help them become financially successful.

Whatever your choice, make sure you are fully informed and can make smart, confident investing decisions with your money.

That'll put you well ahead of many adults out there as well!

If Debt Happens ... Deal with It

D ebt happens. If you get into deep debt, don't panic. Take a deep breath. And read on.

It can be really hard to break free from a debt spiral. It's just borrow-and-spend, borrow-more-and-spend again. This cycle starts by borrowing more than you can pay back, then a little more, then a little more. Eventually you have to face the fact that you're sinking, along with the payments you probably can't keep up with.

None of us want to find ourselves in this vicious cycle. However, debt spirals happen all too often in college because students don't quite have enough to get by on, or they don't quite know how to handle the money they do have.

Worst thing you can do in a debt spiral? Freeze up, stick your head in the sand like an ostrich, and pretend that if you can't see it, it isn't happening.

There are other options.

The tips in this book can help you save money to start paying back the debt, so you'll eventually break the cycle. Aggressively track your debt during the payoff period by following these steps:

- Pick the method that works best for you to track your debt: Create an excel spreadsheet, use a debt payoff app or a useful calculator (i.e. Bankrate.com).
- Fill it out every month until the debt is paid off.
- Keep a close eye on credit card interest rates to make sure they don't jump up unexpectedly. If they do, call and ask if they will lower the rate. If not, transfer your balance to

another credit card with a lower interest rate.

- Put any extra cash flow (income) toward your principal.
- Don't put additional charges onto your credit cards if you've had trouble with debt in the past. Cut up those cards, put them in the freezer, or burn them—take your pick.

Work hard to pay off the debt, and then move forward living on an all-cash budget. If you don't have an online app or program that can help you organize your credit card payments, I have included one at the back of the book in Appendix B.

Hitting the Shops

PRACTICE THE 15-MINUTE AND 1-DAY TESTS

You're used to tests, right? So what's one or two more? The "15-minute test" is a simple, effective way of weeding those frivolous, budget-murdering impulse purchases out of your life. Here's how it works:

You're in a store. Your eyes fall on an item that may not be an absolute necessity. But you really want it. It feeeeeeeels like a necessity. And yet, as we all know, feelings can deceive. Here's the test: Walk out of that store, go into another one, or just wander around for fifteen minutes. Don't really think about the item. At the end of the time, ask yourself if you really want it, or have you already forgotten about it? If you've forgotten it, that item just flunked the test. A+ to you!

If you're still thinking about it, evaluate whether or not this item is a true *need* versus a *want*. Ask yourself these questions:

- Can you afford this purchase?
- Does it fit into your budget?
- If you can't afford it, how will you pay for it?
- How will buying it affect other areas of your spending?

The fifteen minutes give you time to contemplate your decision and not make an impulsive purchase. Again, high marks to you.

Try the "1-day test" for online purchases. If you stumble onto a website with no intention of purchasing anything, yet before you know it your shopping cart is overflowing, wait one entire day! If you remember to go back the next day *and* you can afford this purchase *and* it fits in your budget, great. Purchase it.

For me, at least 95% of the time I forget about the item until days later. Considering how easily I forgot about it, how badly did I really want it?

This simple test has saved me thousands of dollars on items I didn't necessarily need and didn't even really want. Impulse control is a great skill to cultivate. Your budget, your bank account, and your already over-stuffed closet will thank you.

Shop Before You Drop

A major plus of modern life: there's always a better deal, especially on the internet. It just takes some digging to find it. Many websites today offer free shipping. If not, search for promo codes or coupons offering free shipping for that website or a certain percentage off.

Instead of buying the first item you see, get the SKU number (item number) and type it in online, along with the product's name or manufacturer's name. Take some time to find the cheapest possible site to buy it from. If you don't usually do this, you might be shocked at the differences in price for one item.

Websites such as Amazon.com, eBay.com, or Overstock.com offer significant discounts compared to department store prices.

It takes time and patience to stay within your budget, especially when your schedule is crammed with classes and social events. But life will always be like that.

So start your scavenger hunt now for the best price on everything you buy.

PURCHASE SCHOOL SUPPLIES ON AN "AS NEEDED" BASIS

Unless you're in an art class, you'll rarely need more than a notebook and a pencil for any class. Even if the syllabus says you need certain supplies, wait until you receive the particular assignment requiring them before making any purchases.

One student's biology lab syllabus asked for a dissection kit. He bought the $40 kit that same day. When it was time for the dissection, the instructor said the department had a set of dissection tools, so the students did not need to buy the set. Since it was already weeks past the return date, the student was stuck with an expensive dissection kit he never used.

#DollarHack #1: Is there a dollar store near you? Check out their school supply sections and prepare to be amazed. Usually, you can find all the basics you need.

#DollarHack #2: Don't be fooled by a store that has the word "dollar" in its name. I'm talking about the real deal, the kind of store where NOTHING costs more than one measly dollar.

#DollarHack #3: Once you see that every single item in the store—large or small—costs only one little dollar, you might lose all control. Do not defeat the entire purpose of shopping there by filling your cart with everything you see, in every color it comes in, because, "Hey, it's only a dollar."

BOOKS, BOOKS, BOOKS!

Never buy new. Not ever. I'm not kidding. New books are shockingly, ridiculously expensive. To avoid this massive budget destroyer, see if your college has an unofficial Facebook page where students sell used books for cheap. Amazon.com (especially great if you have their Prime membership so the shipping is free), Half.com (an eBay company), and Chegg.com will soon become your favorite websites.

They'll rent you a textbook for the entire semester at a dramatically lower price. You have the potential to save thousands of dollars. As long as you are proactive and shop around, you probably can get almost every book you need for a huge discount.

Also, the more students you're friends with, the more likely you'll find someone willing to sell their old books to you at a heavily-discounted *friend-rate*, or even at no cost.

#LibraryHack: Check to see if the school library has the textbook you need. Use those books for free and don't spend a dime on textbooks.

Who's your book daddy now?

SHOPPING FOR CLOTHING

D id I hear you sigh? Is that because shopping is usually a happy and exciting subject, and you now suspect that after you read this, your life will change forever? Or at least for four years? You're right.

Shopping for clothes becomes a little more challenging in college, without Mom and her trusty credit card. If you move to a new town and realize your look is out of style or doesn't quite work (which happened to me going from the Central Valley to the Bay Area in California), you might realize your image and your wardrobe need an update. But, there's no money to make it happen.

Brand name clothing is expensive; even shopping at Target might spell budgetary disaster. If Macklemore doesn't even want to cough up "fifty dollars for a t-shirt," you probably don't either. Take a page out of the hip-hop artist's songbook and head to the thrift shop or consignment shop.

Many people have never shopped in these types of stores and are freaked out at the idea of it. Yes, almost all the clothes you'll find in these places have been worn … horrors! … by someone else. Yes, anything you buy there has got to be cleaned before you wear it.

And yet, you can put together a fantastic wardrobe filled with new-looking, well-made, stylish, and sometimes even designer stuff, if you're willing to give it a try. All for pennies on the dollar of what you'd pay for the same items new.

All you need to do is get comfy with the idea of wearing used clothes. Which, frankly, once you see the price tag, is not hard to do.

If that's a no-go situation for you, there are other ways to get your style on for less. Scour the internet for clothing deals, but only if you're sure of your size. There are loads of killer discounts online. However, if you're stuck returning the item and have to pay shipping both ways, then it's not worth the deal.

#SwapHack: Don't forget your friends, who might all be in the same sartorial situation. Organize a clothing swap with the girls in your dorm or your sorority sisters. Freshen up your closet for no money at all, and get great feedback on your look.

Simply have everyone go through their closet and bring along all the items they're ready to swap, put 'em all together in one room, and let the "shopping" begin. Leftover clothes can be donated to charity.

FILL THE PANTRY WITHOUT BREAKING THE BANK

U nless you are in the dorms with a full meal plan, eating will require cooking. Your cooking. Are you making your own meals? If so, buying groceries and paper goods in bulk from a big-box membership warehouse market like Costco or Sam's Club is the way to go.

These markets are great for stocking your kitchen to the brim at a relatively low cost. Even better if you have room- mates who share your taste buds or love to cook for the house. Chip in for the yearly membership fee and stock up.

But even at a great price, think before you splurge. Sometimes it's a waste of money to buy from wholesale clubs. Before you haul out that 25 pound bag of onions, consider how much of it your household can really use. Remember, fresh food does not stay fresh forever. Unless you host Taco Tuesday for your entire fraternity, those onions will grow funky shoots and probably rot before you use them up.

Instead, *make like a coupon-clipping mom* and shop around at the local markets, too. Check prices and watch for specials and only buy what you really think you'll use. The savings can be huge!

Many grocery stores have reward cards that give you cash back or additional discounts. Be sure to sign up for those cards *if there is no cost involved*.

GET THEE TO THE DOLLAR & GENERAL STORES

We talked about the "real" dollar store already, but there are lots of other stores that call themselves dollar stores. Things might cost more than one dollar, but they offer great savings on all kinds of items you might need on a day-to-day basis.

If you've never been in one of these stores and there's one close to your campus, give it a try. Bet you'll be shocked by all the goodies they sell at these places.

Before I buy a product, I always check the local Dollar Tree or Dollar General to see if they have it. These stores are stocked to the brim with all kinds of great stuff: cool kitchen utensils and cleaning supplies, enough party decorations to sink the Titanic, great greeting cards, even really cheap food and candies.

Yes, candy!

The dollar store or local general store also sells basic school supplies at a major discount, compared to the campus bookstore.

Need a unique Halloween costume without breaking the bank? Check if the dollar store has any accessories you can throw together to make it work. Don't forget the craft aisle for paints and the makeup aisle for ... makeup! Doesn't spending $10 on a DIY costume sound more appealing than spending $50 on a prefab one?

Anytime you need to buy something other than a new iPhone, check the dollar store first.

A Grocery List—
Don't Leave Home Without It

When you go grocery shopping, do it with a list. Do I see you rolling your eyes? Let's get one thing straight. Lists rock! Your grocery list will keep you from accidentally buying the same stuff you already have at home, buying stuff you probably won't use, and wasting those precious pennies that could be used for lots of other fun things.

If you really want to go all "*frugalista*," write out a meal plan for the week so you have a good idea of how much food to purchase. Watching food go bad in your fridge is … well, it's just bad.

Think of your grocery list as a secret weapon that will defend your budget in several ways:

- It will keep you from forgetting things you need, so you don't go to get a glass of milk during a 2 a.m. cram session and find out you have none.

- It will keep you more focused and shorten the length of time you're in the store.

- It will help keep you from impulse buying … because you're going to pinky swear with yourself that if it isn't on the list, *it's not going in the cart*.

- With or without a list, please don't buy groceries at a convenience or liquor store. Sorry, 7-Eleven. But these kinds of stores are the most expensive places to buy food and often have price markups significantly greater than a supermarket or wholesale store.

SAVE BIG TIME
WITH GENERIC OR STORE BRANDS

B uying the generic version or store brand name items is one of the easiest, savviest, and simplest ways to save money. These brands sit right next to the name brands on the shelf, inviting price comparisons.

Will the generic cereal taste as good as my Cheerios, you wonder? Will the cheap cough medicine work just as well? Will the generic antiperspirant really stop the sweat?

You'll have to do some experimentation. Higher price does not always mean higher quality. Many items come in generic or store brands; take a look the next time you hit the market.

Even a high-end market like Whole Foods has their own brand, 365, which offers significant savings. In Walmart, check out Equate, their store brand that copies the formulas of popular grooming products, beauty products, even over-the-counter drugs, and sells them for less.

From your favorite box of cereal to your shampoo to your medicine, generic and store brands provide savings in every aisle. If this is a new idea for you, you can ask the sales staff in any big box store or any large supermarket what the names are of their store brands.

In most drugstores, the pharmacist can walk you through the pros and cons of buying a generic medicine. Ask him/ her to show you the ingredient comparison for your peace of mind.

PERILS OF A FULL WALLET AND AN EMPTY STOMACH

Never shop hungry. Shopping hungry leads to impulse buying, because everything looks incredibly, unbearably delicious, and you simply have to have it. You are thinking with your stomach, and your budget is the last thing on your mind.

When I'm hungry, the first thing I do is throw six bags of those pink and white animal crackers into my cart. Who needs that many animal crackers? Not my waist, my butt, my blood sugar, or my budget.

If you shop on a full stomach, you're much more likely to buy less and stay within your budget. This has been researched and proven. It's definitely my experience.

Unless you're heading to Costco when they hand out free food samples on every aisle, plan to have a full belly before heading off to the store.

You know what that means, don't you? It means don't wait to shop till you have absolutely nothing in the cup- boards.

CHOOSE THE RIGHT MEAL PLAN

L iving on campus? Meal plans vary from one campus to the next. If you're going to sign up for one, do some re- search first. Be realistic about how many meals you're willing to eat on campus, then calculate the average cost per meal of each plan.

This way, you can minimize what you're paying per meal and get the most bang for your buck without any waste. For example, if you never eat breakfast, buy a meal plan for two meals a day. If you're planning on getting a part-time job in the evenings and will never be around for dinner, do the same. Don't waste your money on a three-meals-a-day plan you won't take full advantage of.

In addition to meal credits, most colleges also have some form of *meal cash*. This "cash" can only be spent on campus food or certain other places around town.

Sorry, Taco Bell and Pizza Hut are usually not on the list.

The "meal cash" route gives you more flexibility and sometimes the option to buy non-food items as well. Make sure you understand the restrictions and timeline with your meal plan. Also, find out if you can switch to another plan mid-semester, if the one you chose isn't really working for you.

Only buy as much as you'll use. Consider your schedule and your eating habits before making a decision. Wasted meal credits, or wasted "meal cash" is wasted money.

STICK TO CHICKEN

Red meat is expensive. Sigh. Buying it can blow your budget pretty quickly and restrict the total amount of food you can afford. I know a delicious seasoned tri-tip is tempting, but save that order for a special occasion or when a family member takes you out to dinner.

If you've just gotta have red meat, talk to the butcher at your local supermarket and find out what's on sale. Or find the markdown section. Typically, those meats are on sale because they are only a day or two from their expiration dates, so as soon as you get home, fire up that BBQ and enjoy your filet.

LEARN TO ROCK A RICE COOKER

Few meals are cheaper or easier to make than steamed rice. While you don't need a rice cooker to make good rice, it makes the job so much easier. With a rice cooker, all you need is rice and water, and to push the start button and boom, twenty minutes later you're chowing down on per- fectly cooked rice. No mess, no hassle, no burnt pot because you forgot to watch the time, and just one pot to clean. The rice doesn't even stick to it. It's like a cooking miracle.

Eat your rice with chicken or veggies or eggs, in a tortilla or a wrap, so many different ways. If you look online for cheap rice recipes, they'll come up in the thousands.

A rice cooker makes a killer high school graduation gift, so ask for one!

THE GENIUS OF THE CROCK-POT®

Crock-Pot® or other brand of slow cooker is an ab- solute college must. With a slow cooker, you can cook almost anything you want, and like the rice cooker, all you have to do is push the start button. College life is busy, and most days you'll be exhausted after a full day of classes. You won't want to cook. You might not want to cook even without a full day of classes.

But you will be hungry, and that hunger can easily drive you out to a budget-wrecking restaurant. Repeatedly. Cut your hunger off at the pass by planning for it in advance. Throw a bunch of chicken parts, broth, and veggies in your slow cooker before you head off to class. Voila … you'll return to a complete meal, ready for you to dig right in. Don't be surprised when your mouth starts watering as you unlock your front door. Take that, hunger!

Slow cookers make any dish easy to prepare and the cleanup is simple. They're inexpensive, easy to get the hang of, and durable. You don't even need a special slow cooker cookbook be- cause you'll find hundreds, if not thousands, of slow cooker recipes online. Pinterest is one of my favorite places to find great recipes.

The Crock-Pot® and the internet: a match made in culinary heaven.

Before you leave for college, ask your mom, aunt, or grandma for their favorite slow cooker recipes, too.

BYOB (Bring Your Own Bags) to the Grocery Store

In some parts of the country, supermarkets charge a grocery bag fee. A dime or two doesn't sound like much, does it? So what's the big deal?

If you think of how many grocery bags you'll use over the course of your college career—probably a mind boggling amount—this can add up to real money over time, money you might rather spend on something other than a flimsy plastic bag that's already sprung a hole by the time you get it home. Am I right?

Do you really want to waste your money paying for plas- tic or paper bags? Why not just buy reusable bags once, and bring them each time you go? Not to mention, while you're saving your hard earned cash, you're also helping save the environment. And there are all kinds of really cool reusable bags out there, guaranteed to suit your style. Check your supermarket or dollar store for the best bags.

WATCH THE REGISTER DURING CHECKOUT

Cashiers are people, too. You might even be a cashier, and if you are, you know everyone makes mistakes. Whenever you buy something, especially clothing and groceries, check to make sure the register is correct.

Often times there are specials or deals, the register won't automatically mark it down and the cashier has to manually punch in the deal. Cashiers do their best to remember all the deals, but sometimes they accidentally forget to input the sale code and overcharge you. Be aware of what they are typing and watch the register the entire time. You can always ask, "Did you get that sale price?" Do it with a smile so you don't sound like a fussbudget. But that's the right word, because the fuss is all about your budget, and making the most of what you have.

Do you keep a running total in your head as you walk through the market tossing items in your cart? If your total is higher than expected, run through the bill with the cashier. Confirm he/she included your special prices or discounts. After the receipt is printed, step aside from the register and review the numbers.

You might feel awkward and ridiculous, but scan the numbers anyway. If they don't look right, hold your head high, politely approach the cashier, and have him or her fix the error and return your cash.

Keep It Old School —
Collect Loose Change in a Jar

Yeah, it's the jar thing. It's tried and true. Every time you come home, toss your loose change into a jar. Throughout the year, this jar will fill up and become a small emergency fund. Bet you'll be surprised how much loose change can add up over a couple of months. At the end of the year or once the jar is full, take it to a bank and roll the coins. You might walk out with a nice little stash, maybe even several twenties in your hands after nine months of collecting loose change.

PERUSE THE FREE SECTION

L ast I heard, we're still living in the land of the free … free stuff, that is.

It's amazing how much stuff people give away for free, great stuff that might be just what you need, just what you've been wanting but not affording. But how do you find all this primo stuff?

Lots of different ways. Take a look at the free section of Craigslist, for starters. Believe it or not, it's under the section marked *For Sale.* A quick glance this morning showed sev- eral sofas and chairs, a treadmill, free firewood (score!) and loads of older-style TVs.

Does your school have a Facebook page for giveaways or low-priced items? Tons of people are just trying to get rid of stuff and are happy to fill a college student's apartment. Usually, you'll have to pick the item up yourself, so plan to borrow a friend's truck. Of course, you can always ask if the other person is willing to drop it off at your apartment, since you are a struggling student and don't have a car.

Remember, someone else's junk may be your treasure during college. Pass on mattresses or upholstered furniture that might have bed bugs or fleas. You don't want any unin- vited guests in your home.

Cooking, Eating, and Drinking

LEARN TO LOVE HOT SAUCE

On a small, college-style budget, you'll eat many foods that are cheap, salty, bland, nasty, or kind of gross. Sorry, that's college life. You'll be wishing you complimented Mom on her awesome dinners every night, when you discover campus cafeteria food does not taste like a home-cooked meal.

Consider yourself lucky if campus food tastes better than hospital food and set your expectations accordingly.

The secret to making any meal edible? Even kind of enjoyable? Yep, hot sauce. You may gag just thinking about this idea now, but trust me, after a couple months of force feeding yourself tasteless chicken or cooked-to-mush pasta, you'll be jonesing for your sauce of choice.

Find your sauce! For some people, the ultimate food-fixer is teriyaki sauce. Others swear by Tabasco. Others can't get enough of Texas Pete or any of those other bottles covered in warning labels because they are so hot and deadly. Yet others have become addicted to Sriracha.

Will you stay loyal to one, or become a sauce connoisseur with a whole shelf filled with them? Whatever you choose, the sooner you find your sauce, the wider your food options become and the better your meals will taste.

BECOME YOUR OWN GOURMET CHEF

Once you move out of the dorms and into your own apartment, cooking is one of the things you have to do on a daily basis. Yet aside from scrambled eggs, reheat- ing leftovers in the microwave, and perhaps boiling pasta, a shocking number of college students can't cook.

I don't count opening a can of tuna and mixing a glob of mayo in it as cooking. I don't count slathering two slices of bread with peanut butter and jelly as cooking. I'm talking about nice, hot, yummy, soul-feeding food. If you luck out and get a roommate who loves to cook, do the happy dance. I knew a student who had absolutely no idea how to cook when he first moved into his apartment. This poor guy took a chicken breast straight from the freezer and tossed it merrily on the grill. He was surprised and upset when the outside of the chicken was black, but the inside was still frozen. And he was still hungry and getting hungrier.

If you're reading this thinking, "Yowsa, I didn't know you couldn't put a frozen chicken breast on the grill," then it might be time to get your chef on.

Living on your own is the time to learn how to cook for yourself. You can take a cooking class on campus, or maybe ask a culinarily-inclined friend to show you a few things. If you're still at home, shock and delight your mother by asking her to teach you how to make your favorite of her dishes.

Experiment now, before cooking for other people. Besides, even if it turns out disgusting, you can still drown it in hot sauce and it'll be at least as edible as the campus cafeteria food.

If you have space outside your apartment, or a sunny windowsill, plant a few herbs like basil and rosemary. They'll add great flavor to your cooking, you gourmet you.

EAT BEFORE A SPORTING EVENT

We all love hanging with our friends at sporting events, chowing down on a hot dog and a drink. However, the food at sporting events is outrageously priced for most Americans, not to mention poor down-and-out college students.

Make yourself a meal before you go to the event. Fill your belly so full that the aroma of overcooked hot dog and mustard does not even tempt you. The proper pre-game attitude has nothing to do with your team winning, but rather "OMG, I couldn't eat another bite."

You could even go out to eat before going to the event. It will be cheaper, and you'll get more food. Nobody needs to pay $20 for a Ballpark frank and some french fries.

The same rules apply for drinks at sporting events. If you're not careful, one measly sporting event can wreck your budget for the month. No matter which team wins, you will be sorry in the morning.

KNOW YOUR LIMITS WHEN DINING OUT

It's always cheaper to make your meals at home than it is to go out to a restaurant. A real restaurant, that is, not a fastfood drive-through. But man, or college student, cannot live by home cooking alone. Sometimes you will go out.

Stay on budget by ordering an appetizer as opposed to an entrée. Appetizers are cheaper than a full meal, but some of them are also tiny and not enough for a meal. Ask the wait- ress how big it is. Chain restaurants like Chili's and Applebee's frequently have appetizers the size of your apartment. French restaurants do not.

Order an appetizer and a glass of water instead of a soft drink and you can cut your dinner bill almost by half. Yes, I did say water!

Soft drinks are a luxury you cannot afford when you go out to a restaurant. You can save several dollars at every meal by drinking water. If you want more flavor, ask for a wedge of lemon or lime.

If you're of drinking age, buy the cheapest drink they offer. Now is not the time to be "poppin' bottles" of Grey Goose and Patron to impress your friends. Alcohol is highly marked up at restaurants and bars, because that's where they make the most money. Instead, buy a pitcher of Natural Light. Unless you've budgeted for a $10 drink, wait until you get home to enjoy that VO & 7 or vodka tonic.

GET SEPARATE CHECKS

Going out to eat can be tricky when the bill comes. You might wind up paying more than your share if everyone wants to split the bill evenly, and you bought the cheapest food. I suggest telling the people with you that you're on a tight budget. They will understand. No one will think less of you.

Ask the waiter for a separate bill. Splitting the bill ensures you only pay for what you ordered *and* keeps you from looking like a cheapskate. However, some restaurants do not allow bill splitting. Ask before you order to avoid nasty and expensive surprises later.

"Can we get separate checks?" is the perfect question. Trust me, it's one your wait person has heard a billion times before.

If the restaurant will not split the bill, someone in your group who's good with math and didn't drink a pitcher of beer can figure out each person's share at the table. Or, your group could have one person spot the bill, take it home and calculate what each person owes. Ideally, this person will be paid back within one week. Apps like Venmo make it conve- nient and easy to pay back a friend.

THE FREEZER IS YOUR FRIEND

Try not to let food (that you paid for) go to waste. Sure, you're going to be super-busy, and things will come up to keep you away from your refrigerator, sometimes for many meals at a time. Make it a habit to check what's going on in your fridge on a regular basis. Science experiments are gross.

If you know certain foods will expire soon, make it a priority to cook and eat those foods first. The freezer is your savior here. Stash meat that's nearing its expiration date in the freezer if you don't have time to cook it and eat it before it goes bad. Same goes for fruit. If it's over ripe or about to go bad, stick it in the freezer. (In a plastic zip-lock bag.) This will keep it from rotting and then it can be used for delicious smoothies or banana bread.

What about those veggies? If you have a fridge full of vegetables ready to go bad, pull out the slow cooker and make stew for your friends. It only takes a few minutes to find a recipe online that will use up the ingredients in your refrigerator. And if you wind up with way too much stew? Portion it out into plastic containers (get 'em in the dollar store) and throw them in the freezer too.

LEARN TO LOVE LEFTOVERS

L eftovers. Some people love them. Some people hate them. The leftover debate rages on. But as a college student on a budget, learning to get creative with them will save you big bucks and keep you eating well.

Here's how to take leftovers and do something interesting with them. Got any meat leftover from last night's dinner, either home-cooked or eaten out? (You do ask for doggie bags, don't you?) Chop it into small pieces and add it to a pasta sauce. Or add some salsa, wrap it in a tortilla, and call it a burrito.

Leftover veggies? Toss some grated cheese over them and bake till the cheese melts. Leftover rice? Layer it with any other leftovers in a casserole dish, toss on some hot sauce, and voila!

Leftover pizza? I bet I don't have to tell you what to do with that!

It's great to use up your leftovers. They make a quick meal, not much to clean up, and you might even like your new culinary creation so much you'll want to make it from scratch.

BECOME YOUR OWN BARISTA

There's no doubt that a Starbucks Grande skinny vanilla latté extra-hot tastes better than any cup of coffee from my coffee maker. I'm right there with you on this one!

However, most college budgets do not have room for a $5 latté once a day or even once a week. If you decide that really great coffee is going to be your one luxury, your one splurge, and you simply have to have it, evaluate your budget and decide what other expenditures you'll have to decrease. And then ask yourself … is it really worth it?

While you're in the dorms, find an instant coffee or tea your taste buds like. There are many to choose from. Once you move into an apartment, buy a coffee maker. You can explore flavored coffees and creamers to make your coffee a little more exciting. Throw some cinnamon on the top to add a little spice.

Got a birthday coming up? Be wise and go for the prize: ask for one of those shiny, expensive espresso machines.

WATER FILTER

Are you used to grabbing water bottles your parents had conveniently stocked in the refrigerator? Prepare to change your expensive ways.

Americans are obsessed with bottled water. The marketing has gotten very elaborate and a bottle is outrageously expensive. The simple solution? Buy a water filter pitcher that can fit right into your refrigerator. Fill your eco-friendly water bottle from your filtered water and you're ready to go. You'll be saving money while caring for the Earth at the same time.

Or … for something truly different, you could just drink your H2O straight up, right from the tap.

Social Life

It Pays to Play — Greek Life

Go Greek or stay independent? They both have their pros and cons. From a financial standpoint, Greek life might not be in the budget. But from a social perspective, Greek life is a blast and makes a memorable college experience. If Greek life is a priority for you, budget accordingly. There might be other things you'll have to do without to be able to afford it.

Here are a few #GreekSavingHacks:

- Ask your treasurer if the national or local chapter gives any discounts on dues for good grades or other outstanding performance.
- If apparel is not included in your dues, buy the bare minimum. You don't need 27 shirts or tank tops with your organization's name on it. Two or three are acceptable.
- Compare the price of living in the Fraternity/Sorority house to living in an apartment or satellite house. Choose the cheaper (and cleaner and more study- friendly) option.
- Compare meal plans offered by your Greek organization to the cost of buying your own groceries. Once again, pick the cheaper option.
- Instead of buying an outfit for every themed party, ask around to see if any of your brothers or sisters have any extra items you can borrow. If not, hit the thrift store.
- Formals and semi formals are expensive. Limit the ones you attend to your junior and senior years, if you are of drinking age.

Don't Break the Bank on Spring Break

Spring break is a college rite of passage. Spring break trips with your mates are crazy-good fun, filled with lasting memories (perhaps including things you'd really rather forget). However, they can bust the budget and break the bank. Saving for a spring break trip will take discipline and patience. Every month, put a portion of your funds aside for this trip. Spring break trips are worth the price tag, but only if you leave your vacation without debt.

Here's my budget-friendly suggestion. Only take one spring break trip during your college career. Your trip doesn't have to be Cabo, Vegas, or Lake Havasu to be a great time. It's just as much about the people you're with as the places you go. Use the budgeting tips listed throughout this book to save up the money you'll need, and enjoy the fruits of your frugality.

I recommend a separate savings account for your vaca- tion fund. (Assuming your bank won't charge you a fee.)

Separating vacation money from day-to-day living expenses is imperative, so you can see what you have saved and prevent those funds from being spent on supermarket splurges.

GET CREATIVE—DATING ON A BUDGET

Dating on a miserly income is tricky. You want to impress. You want to show your date a great time. But there are ways to take Ms. or Mr. Hottie out on a cheap date, without appearing cheap or clueless:

- Dinner and a movie is your basic, traditional kind of date. Always nice when you can catch a cheap matinee, but definitely expensive otherwise. If the only place you can afford to take your date is KFC, perhaps it's time for something a bit more creative and a lot more intimate. (Although I do really love their biscuits!) Ask your roommates to leave for the night and cook dinner yourself. Prepare everything beforehand but cook it together. Dazzle your date with either your newfound cooking skills, or your sense of humor about your lack of cooking skills.

- After dinner, instead of going out to the movies with their outrageous six-dollar small popcorns, watch one on Netflix and microwave popcorn—with real butter, of course. You're classy! In total, this date shouldn't cost you more than $20. (Assuming you aren't so anx- ious to impress that you go berserk in the supermarket, buying every gourmet treat in sight.)

- Discover the fun of daytime dates. Hiking or biking to a nearby beach, lake, river, or mountain peak are great ways to stay active and get to know someone in more natural ways. These types of dates are free, fun, and can be really romantic.

- Grab your snacks, fill a picnic basket and head to the beach, mountaintop, or lake; watch a sunset.
- Throw in a group date every once in a while, even if you don't like his/her friends. Your partner will appreciate your openness and flexibility.
- If you have a bunch of friends who are dating too, host a game night. Ask friends to bring their games to add to your stash. Cards Against Humanity will provide hours of completely free laughs.
- Find out what free events are happening in town or on campus. Take your date to a First Friday Artwalk, an Octoberfest celebration, whatever your town is offering. Find out when the free days are at the zoo (great date!), the aquarium, or the local museums.

SPREAD THE LOVE, SHARE THE PARTIES

Are you the organizer of your group, the one who gets everyone together on Friday night? The one with all the great ideas? You will definitely be popular ... but make sure those great ideas don't sink you in a financial hole.

Typically, the organizer gets stuck hosting all the parties because they were his/her idea. Unfortunately, hosting just one party can throw your budget out of whack for the rest of the month, even set you back a couple of months (especially if things get a bit crazy, the cops are called, and you wind up with a noise violation).

To maximize the fun, yet minimize how much that fun costs you, make a firm resolve to throw only one party *at your place* per semester. Instead, why not rotate party loca- tions among your friends?

#PartyHatHack: Save all decorations and leftover paper plates and stuff like that for the next party. And wherever the party goes down, always be respectful of the neighbors.

BEFRIEND A SOCIAL BEE OR PARTY ANIMAL

Some people are the life of any party; the connectors, the social bees, the party animals. They know everyone. They know everything that's going on. They know how to have a good time, all the time. They're up for anything and delighted to bring you along for the ride. The more, the merrier!

There are many advantages to making friends with some- one like this, especially if you aren't quite that outgoing your- self. Your uber-social friend will likely throw lots of parties, and you'll be invited. Insta-social life!

Ms. or Mr. Mega-social will introduce you to all kinds of new people to widen your social circles. While your social life will thrive, your social budget will wither if you are not careful.

Social bees have a million ideas for things to do. They're up for anything, anytime. "No" does not seem to be in their vocabulary. But it needs to be in *yours*. Of course, you don't want to sound dull, boring, pathetic, or cheap. But you don't want to blow your budget either.

Practice these lines; some are straight, some are funny.

Adapt to fit your style:

"I'm going to pass on that. Next time, though." "Sorry, dude. Too rich for this pauper's blood."

"Let me get back to you after I make my first million." "Sounds amazing. Can I get a rain check?"

"Oooooh, if only I didn't have that (fill in the blank) test tomorrow. I really need to study."

"Wow. I want to hear all about it. Call me!"

Get Involved in a Setup

Helping friends set up (or clean up) for a social event is the college equivalent of treating them to dinner. It is a major step in a new friendship. If you help your friend set up for a party or other kind of event, you'll always be invited back. You'll most likely get free entry, a cold drink, free meal, and most important, you'll be known as a cool, stand-up kind of person who is always willing to help.

Helping friends who are organizing campus events can help you get involved and perhaps get in for free, depending on the event.

There are many areas where friends might need an ex- tra hand: moving into a new apartment, going to pick up some furniture they just bought, needing a ride somewhere, needing a wingman, or just needing a warm body for moral support. They won't all save you money directly, the way helping friends set up for events will, but most people will be happy to repay the favor when you need one.

Decorations on the Cheap

Sometimes you'll want to host a party that stands out, the kind people can't wait to come to and can't stop raving about after they leave. Whether this party is for a club, a frat, a special event, or just because you feel like it, decorations are one of the things that make all the difference. And of course, decorations can cost a pretty penny, so scavenging for them can end up saving you hundreds of dollars. Here are some ways to get cost-effective decorations:

- This isn't exactly a decoration, but it's important. Parties can and do get wild. Things will spill. Mud will be tracked in. Food will be ground into your rug. Don't lose your apartment deposit over a ruined carpet. Ask a local carpeting place if they have any old carpets or remnants they're willing to give away, or put down heavy plastic.
- Get on Pinterest and look up party decorations. Prepare to have your mind blown with all kinds of fun and unique ideas that will really make your party, on the cheap.
- Check out your local dollar store. You're probably a regular there by now, right? They have aisles of decorations that could spruce up your party.
- To build something fun like a bar, an arbor, or a sign, search around town for piles of scrap wood. Go to your local dump and ask if you can have any scrap wood that hasn't been processed yet. They'll most likely let you take it if you're quick and don't get in the way of their operation.

KEEP IT DOWN! AVOID NOISE VIOLATIONS

A noise violation can damage your finances, ruin your relationship with your neighbors, and put your house on a watch list in your college town. You want to avoid this at all costs (pun intended), especially because most parents aren't willing to pick up this kind of tab. The cost of the ticket var- ies depending on your city and the time of day, *number of offenses, and type of noise violation.*

Be aware of the noise level during your parties. If you can't hear yourself think, it's probably too loud. Keep par- ties behind closed doors, speakers facing inward, windows closed. Consider hanging blankets on thin walls to dampen the ambient noise leaking out. Find out if your town has noise ordinances and what time the music needs to turn way, way down. Find out the easy way, by checking into it before the party. Not the hard way, when the cops come pounding on your door.

Make the effort to be on friendly terms with your neigh- bors. If you are throwing a bash, let them know things might be a bit loud Friday night. Perhaps, if appropriate, even invite them. People at the party will not be calling the police to complain about the party! Clever, right?

There are many advantages to getting to know your neighbors. At least a little bit.

Few things enrage people more than trying to sleep with some- one else's party blasting in their ears. If your neighbors know you and like you even a little bit, they will often come to you before turning to the authorities, saving you from strained relationships and battered budgets.

If the police do show up at your door, be respectful. No attitude! Apologize for the disturbance. Tell them it won't happen again. Immediately lower the music or whatever other noise is going on.

LAND OF THE FREE (EVENTS)

Most colleges offer your new favorite type of events—free ones. Concerts, movie nights, entertainers, mixers, and of course, a plethora of different sporting events. Go to as many as you can! They are free with your student ID.

Look on your school website, Facebook page, or in your school newspaper for a complete list of upcoming events. Check out all kinds of stuff you never would have been in- terested in before. You might just find a new friend or a new passion.

Your school's town will hold free events as well, including farmer's markets, carnivals, concerts, or public movie showings, parades, and festivals. The bigger the town, the more free events. Look up your local newspaper, town website, or Parks and Recreation Department website to find information on upcoming events.

Here's to Happy Hour

If you're going out to lunch or dinner with friends, I recommend hitting your restaurant of choice at Happy Hour—Margarita Monday, Taco Tuesday, Wine Wednesday—you get the point. Happy Hour is the best bang for your buck. The Happy Hour menu is not extensive, but the prices are low and the drinks are reasonable, too.

Call first and make sure the place you want to go has a Happy Hour and confirm the time period.

Make sure to ask for the Happy Hour menu, not the regular one.

#HappyHourHack: Watch the clock when ordering. Time flies when you're having fun and prices fly when Happy Hour is over. A drink that was $1 until 6pm might skyrocket up to $7 when ordered at 6:01pm. If you're not careful with the time, your Happy Hour might turn really unhappy when you get the bill.

Day-to-Day Living

STUDENT DISCOUNTS ABOUND

Your student ID gives you purchasing super-powers. Many establishments in college towns have some form of student discount. There are even lots of online retailers who do as well, so look for them. Check out sites like Gift Card Granny.com, that offer student discounts as well. Always ask before you buy anything anywhere, in any kind of store or fast food place or regular restaurant, because many of these discounts are not advertised.

The worst that can happen is they say, "No, sorry." Never be afraid or embarrassed to ask, "Do you have a student discount?" This question can be your college mantra. Asking does not make you cheap, it makes you smart.

Local businesses thrive on student traffic.They understand students are on tight budgets. Scan the internet for "student discounts" to find all the stores that offer reductions. Check your school website to see if they list local businesses with discounts.

If someone is offering you a discount, take advantage of it!

INVITE FAMILY TO VISIT

Homesick? Missing your old friends, your sibs, your dad's bad jokes, and your mom's smile? No money to get home for a visit? No worries. Make them visit you!

Gone are the childish high-school days where you wouldn't be caught dead with your parents. In college, parents and family seem a whole lot cooler. Absence really does make the heart grow fonder. And best friends from home who drop in for the weekend can be the perfect antidote to school pressures, loneliness, or social stress. These visits rock because:

- It's great to see family & friends, especially if you don't have the money to go home and you're kinda homesick.
- You start to appreciate everything others have done for you and begin to realize how financially difficult putting you through school really is.
- Your relationship with your parents may begin to turn from parent-child to something more like a friendship.
- When relatives visit, they recognize your poor-student status and will often buy you dinner, restock your pan- try, ask if you need new clothes, or give you a little bit of spending cash. They feel good, you feel amazing. Win-win!

Clearly communicate how often you'd like people to visit and which are the best times, so everyone is on the same page. Sometimes family members can "over-visit" and be an annoyance or "under-visit" and hurt your feelings. Let them know what works for you.

WORK IT OUT AT THE FREE CAMPUS GYM

L et's focus on "the other six-pack." Gym memberships are pretty pricey. But you don't need all the bells and whistles of a pricey gym; you simply need a place to work out, a place to help you and your budget stay healthy and fit together.

The good news is that most campuses have a gym included in your tuition. Yes, they are crowded at times, but stay focused on the free aspect. Find a time that works best in your schedule. It's a cliché, sure, but it's also true that the gym is a great place to meet attractive members of either sex who are likeminded about staying fit.

Why wouldn't you go?

NEVER LET 'EM SEE YOU SWEAT

We're about to take a dive into controversy. To wear or not to wear sweats to class—that is the question. Many students wear sweatpants and a t-shirt pretty much every day, especially to the early morning classes. This is not a fashion statement; it's just easy and cheap, it maximizes the time you can stay in bed before getting ready for the day, and is ridiculously comfortable.

But is it too comfortable? Are you too comfortable? *USA Today* ran an article titled "5 Reasons to Stop Wearing Sweatpants to Class." Here's a quote: "… studies show students who dress well for exams have greater confidence and performance."1

Some professors feel wearing sweats is perfectly accept- able, except for test days. Others find it lazy and disrespectful. Why not gauge the sweat climate on your campus, maybe even ask a re- spected professor or two what they think? You'll show yourself as someone thoughtful and interested in both your education and your professional image, and make a great impression on your teachers.

If you're wearing sweats because everyone else is, or be- cause there's just no money in your budget for better clothes, remember you can find great deals for next to nothing at local thrift or con- signment shops.

IT SMELLS

L et's talk laundry. Aren't you excited? Fact is, unless you live in your own apartment with your own washer and dryer, washing your clothes is a big ex- pense. I'm a big fan of hygiene, so don't get me wrong—I am not encouraging anyone to wear stained or smelly clothes! Gross! Unacceptable!

But you don't have to go overboard in the other direction, either. If it's not dirty and it doesn't smell, then why clean it? Here's a tip. If you take your clothes off at night and toss them in a heap on the floor, you won't want to put them on again even if they aren't dirty. If you throw them neatly over a chair, they'll have a much more approachable look to them. There are many kids who get to college having never done their own laundry in their lives. Believe it or not, like all other activities, laundry is not without its pitfalls.

If you don't know what you're doing, you might ruin your clothes, costing you hundreds of dollars to replace.

Here are some more tips:

- One red sock can dye a whole load of laundry pink. These days more and more clothing is colorfast, but not all. Red clothes are the biggest offender. Until you're sure they won't bleed, only wash them with other dark colors.
- Careful with that bleach! Too much will weaken the fabric or eat right through it, leaving holes.
- Buy detergent pods instead of normal liquid or powdered detergent. They are foolproof, preventing you from over or under soaping. They minimize the chance of a mess,

and keep you from mistaking bleach for detergent (a mistake that I guarantee you will see or hear about at least once during your first year of college) and ruining a sizeable chunk of your wardrobe in one short cycle.

- If you have your own washer/dryer, save money by using cold water and the shortest cycle (unless clothes are really dirty). Only do full loads.

#LaundryHack: Avoid paying for laundry by doing it at someone else's house. Clever, right? I babysat all through college. This was a great side job that generated spending money and saved me money too, because most families allowed me to wash my clothes at their house while I was babysitting.

If you have any kind of job with access to a washer and dryer, it doesn't hurt to ask.

BEWARE THE DRYER

The dryer is a ruthless beast that must be respected and understood. Without proper knowledge of its evil ways, it will destroy your clothes in a heartbeat. I can't tell you how many t-shirts my dryer has turned into crop tops.

Which may be cool for girls, since crop tops are always hot, but for you guys? Not so much.

Let's not even talk about how many pajama bottoms have been reduced to crop pants or the warm winter sweaters that shrank up to three-quarter sleeved and not so warm. All from the dryer.

The savviest solution? Take it old school with a real clothesline. Yep, I'm saying to hang dry your clothes. (Still a common sight all over Europe, by the way.)

You won't have to pay for the dryer. Your jeans won't get too short, requiring you to buy new ones. You won't get any dryer burn marks (yes, that's a thing). Your t-shirts and other knits won't get all faded and pilled and shabby, requiring new clothes you can't afford.

Just find a spot on your property that gets some good sunlight, and tie a piece of string between two trees. If you can't find any place for a clothesline, you can buy an inexpensive drying rack or hang your best stuff on hangers around your house. This could save you hundreds of quarters and keep your clothes fitting just like when you bought them.

If you absolutely must use the dryer … use it on a lower heat setting for clothing safety.

CLOTHING SWAPS ARE HOT

Your mom taught you it's important to share, right? Put that vital social skill to great use when it comes to your wardrobe.

In high school, I had one friend I regularly shared and swapped clothes with. Once I was in the dorms, I had 50! This exponentially increases your current wardrobe at no cost to you.

Closet space in the dorms is limited. When I say limited, I'm not kidding. You'll be lucky to fit five t-shirts, a few pairs of jeans, two sweatshirts and sweats, and a few dresses for parties. That's it!

That might be fine for you guys, but torture for the girls. When it comes to expanding your college wardrobe without spending any money, this is where you can really benefit by being both a borrower and a lender.

So girls, talk to your roommates or sorority sisters to see if they're willing to share clothes. Remember to take good care of your friends' stuff, and return it promptly, clean and in the same condition you borrowed it in. If you do damage or ruin something, quickly replace it or offer to pay for the article of clothing. This will ensure that your friends continue to let you borrow their clothes and shoes and bags and jewelry and all that other good stuff.

Unsubscribe to Magazines
and Shopping Websites

Say goodbye to all your *Glamour*, your *InStyle*, your *Maxim*, even your *Car and Driver*, because these sub- scriptions are a luxury you can no longer afford. They cost money (and tempt you to buy the luscious things they advertise.)

If you want to flip through magazines, enjoy the ones at the salon when you're getting your hair cut. Or go to the library. They usually have every magazine on Earth. You can even borrow back issues, but not the current month's issue. If one of your friends gets magazines, ask if you can have them when he/she is done.

Now, on to shopping websites. We love them dearly. But if you're receiving emails advertising sales and bargains and deals of the day and new designers and anything else that is not FREE from shopping websites, unsubscribe immediately.

Students, save yourselves!

The best way to avoid email shopping temptation is to unsub- scribe from these advertising emails.

No bargain is a real bargain if it blows your budget. No sale is a good sale if it tempts you astray, filling your already too small closet with things you really didn't need and definitely couldn't afford.

Students, be strong!

EMBRACE DIY PAMPERING

L adies, I'll bet you already know the price of a mani/pedi in your town. Of course, you need your nails to look great at all times. I'd never suggest otherwise.

And the occasional facial is a beauty must.

But instead of going to a salon or a spa, why not give yourself a spa treatment, or get a group of girlfriends together to give each other one? This is one of the most fun girls' night outs you can have. Or should I say, girls' night ins!

All kinds of fantastic smelling masques and every imagin- able color of nail polish can be found on the cheap at local drugstores.

If you've always had your mani done in a salon, the sheer variety of fancy polishes, decals, paint pens, and custom nail painting kits in your local Walmart or Walgreens will blow your mind!

If you're hosting the spa night or the mani/pedi party, have your friends bring magazines and snacks and their favorite spa stuff. This can also give you the fashion mag fix you've been jonesing for, if you followed the advice in the previous tip and got rid of all your magazine subscriptions.

ALWAYS USE A COUPON

This is self-explanatory. The more coupons you use, the more money you save. (Well, unless you are buying things you didn't need in the first place, just because you have a coupon. Don't do that!)

Websites like Coupons.com will help you save. Look for a coupon code before you make any purchase online; all it takes is a little Googling.

Or do it the simple way with one of those great money saving coupon apps on your phone. Look up coupon apps and prepare to save.

Many big stores have their own coupon apps as well. Which are the stores you shop in the most? Go online and find out if they have a coupon app, then when you're in the store, use it to save!

Avoid Adopting a Four-Legged Friend

Many students are tempted to get a dog in college, es- pecially if they are a bit homesick for the pooch they left behind. And anyway, who doesn't want to hang out with man's best friend?

Convince one of your roommates to get a dog instead. This gives you all the doggy fun without any of the financial burden. The average monthly cost of owning a dog could be more than your dining out or clothing allowance.

Are you willing to give up another item in your budget for a pet?

These are all the costs you will have to absorb with a dog: purchase price or adoption, heartworm treatments, vaccines, flee medications, veterinarian expenses, food, bed, collar, leash, toys, treats, and bones. Don't forget, you'll be waving bye-bye to your apartment deposit if your new puppy takes to peeing on your apartment carpet. Not to mention the awkwardness and possible expense if your dog chews your roommate's new boot instead of his chew toy, or eats the crotch out of her pajama bottoms.

Are you "dog desperate?" Why not volunteer one morning a month in a local shelter, or pick up dog-sitting jobs for a local family and make some money while getting your dog-bonding time.

USE THE 5-MINUTE-SHOWER RULE

A water bill is something many kids have never seen before going off to college. Most of them are not happy to see it when it shows up to their new apartment or shared house. It can be shockingly high.

Slash your water bill big-time with a timer! Find one in the local dollar store and stash it in the bathroom.

Before stepping into the shower, set your trusty timer for five minutes and not a second more.

"I need more than five minutes worth of water," you cry. Try this attitude adjustment. Instead of water, picture money flowing out of the faucet head and right down the drain. And try this tip, ladies: when shaving your legs, turn off the water and just let it drip to rinse your razor.

If all your roommates agree to this rule, your water bill will shrink dramatically. If you have roommates that stick their nose up at this idea, explain your budget, tempt them with what they might do with the money saved, and then hand them this book. Everyone loves to find ways to stretch their dollars, including your roomies.

REDUCE, REUSE, RECYCLE

Recycling is a great way to make a little extra dough. I'm talking about the C word: Cans. Soda cans, juice cans, beer cans, iced tea cans, and soup cans. Americans discard millions of tons of aluminum each year, much of it in the form of cans. The same cans which can be found in abun- dance on college campuses and probably in your house, as well.

Have a separate trash bag or bin for your recycling. Motivate your roommates to participate by sharing the proceeds with the whole house. The money can be used for treats, such as a monthly pizza night. Great incentive, right?

Once you have a few full bags, go to your local recycling center and turn in the cans. It won't be all that much, but every dollar counts.

WHO BUYS MUSIC ANYMORE?

The days of buying particular songs or entire albums are essentially over ... at least until you graduate. Think of all the other things that you could buy or do with that money!

I know you may think you NEED your music; you can- not survive without it. Music is important to most of us. But instead of buying songs, download a free music app like Pandora or Spotify. These apps let you wirelessly stream music to your phone for free, essentially eliminating the need for you to purchase music.

Stop Thieves from Taking Your Stuff

Every college campus seems to have its share of theft. Sad, but true. When you're on a tight budget, there's no spare cash lying around to buy a new laptop if yours is stolen. Or your iPhone. Or your pricey textbooks. Or your anything.

Take the necessary steps to protect yourself and your valuables. Most likely you aren't going to catch a thief in the act. Instead, deter thieves from stealing your possessions with this great invention called the lock. Use it. Lock your front door. Lock up your bike. Lock your windows. Lock your car. Did you know you can even lock your laptop? It might sound a bit drastic, but why not get a room lock? This way, even if a roommate leaves the front door open, your things will be inaccessible to thieves.

Boring cliché that definitely holds true in this case: Better safe than sorry.

Housing

Make Your House a Home

Even cheap furniture is expensive, and furniture from Target or Ikea can be way out of your range. It can easily cost thousands of dollars to completely furnish your apartment or shared house. But it doesn't have to. Not if you put your creative, scavenger, and treasure hunting skills to work. Look around your campus for old furniture near dumpsters. This is especially fruitful at the beginning and end of the school year, when people are moving around. Someone else's trash could be your treasure. Thoroughly clean any upholstered furniture before bringing it into your house. You don't want any unwanted pets making an appearance. Rent a steamer and use it liberally; steam kills everything.

- Ask relatives or neighbors if they have any old furniture they want to get rid of. Most people have at least one unwanted piece of furniture taking up space in their attic or basement.
- Check out nearby garage or estate sales. They may have posters, furniture, or paintings to give your house some personality.
- Go to nearby furniture stores and ask if they have any refurbished or imperfect items that they are willing to get rid of for free or sell at a discount.
- Hit the thrift shop or consignment store. Again, clean the items before bringing them into your house.
- Check Facebook for school groups with Free and For Sale group pages where students are giving stuff away for free or selling it at low prices.
- Remember the Free section on Craigslist.

Go Paperless—Plates, That Is

When you make the big transition from dormitory life to apartment life, you make another big transition to adulthood. The first few years, your apartment will probably consist of odds and ends and other people's discards. You might have gotten used to using paper plates and paper cups and even plastic silverware, but this is expensive over time.

Go for the real deal instead.

Before heading off to school, ask parents or relatives for old dishes, silverware, furniture, lamps, basically anything they're willing to part with that you might need. Make some genuinely productive use of social media and post about what you need.

Then, make a list of *what you have* and *what you need*. Once you have your list together, call your roommates and decide on the items you still need to fill your apartment. Between the lot of you and your supportive families, you probably will be able to fill in most, if not all, of the gaps. If you still don't have everything you need, remember the Free section on Craigslist, the thrift store, and that old life-saver, the dollar store.

All the things you need to turn your apartment into a real home *will* add up to a small fortune, but you are much too clever to pay that fortune. In this case, fortune favors the thrifty!

FIND BRANDS THAT CATER
TO COLLEGE STUDENTS

If you can't find the items you need for free, shop around in August and September when the Back-to-School specials are running at all the big retailers. Many large retailers put together packages specifically for college students. Check out Target's Room Essentials. They have all the items you need to furnish your dorm, apartment, or house at a cost-effective price. These items include bedding sets, silverware and other kitchen stuff, lamps, dressers, tables, and even some furniture. Try to find a coupon online before you buy.

Walmart and Kohl's and many other retailers also offer special college bedding sets and other things designed for tiny dorm rooms.

JUST SAY NO TO ELECTRICITY

U nless you go to school in the desert, skip the air conditioning. Get a bandana to keep sweat from dripping in your eyes, and get used to hanging around in your underwear (and your bandana). Think liberated. Think counterculture. Think laid-back hippie.

Unless you go to school in the Arctic, keep the heater off as well. Wear leggings under your jeans or stay wrapped in a blanket with your hands clenched on a mug of hot tea at all times. Think cozy!

Okay, I'm exaggerating. But just a wee bit.

Fact is, heating and cooling cost a bundle. If you can handle being a little too hot or a little too cold, you'll save a bundle. Guaranteed.

What? Your roommates insist on heat? What a bunch of wimps! It's time for a house meeting to decide what temperature you'll set the thermostat to. Be polite, but make them realize how easy it is to bundle up indoors and how much money you all can save if you keep the thermostat even five degrees lower.

If your roommates insist on using the heater, decide if they will pay a greater percentage of the heating bill. But approach that subject with caution and your best discretion. It might not go over well. It might not be worth it.

Did your dad always nag you to turn off the lights and electronics when you left a room? Dad wasn't just being cheap. Okay, he really was being cheap, and now it's your turn.

I'm not asking you to live like you're back in the Stone Age, just be conscious of your electricity use. By following these rules, you can save big on your electricity bill.

Leave House Phones at Home

Do you really need a house phone when you have a cell phone? If you get cable (and you know I don't recommend that!) the cable company will try to bundle in a house phone. Don't let them. Be strong.

House phones are a waste of money unless the bundled price makes the phone free. Check and recheck before accepting this deal.

Try to save money with your smartphone options, also. Do you really need unlimited data? Save money by changing this feature.

PASS ON CABLE

In this era of streaming television, can't you get by without cable? After all, you'll be spending a majority of the time you are in your dorm or apartment studying.

If you have to have your shows, Netflix is way cheaper than cable, and it allows you to binge-watch entire seasons of shows at a time. On second thought, maybe that's not such a good idea.

In any case, skip cable, and use the money you save for a subscription to Netflix and Hulu, along with a Roku or other device to stream shows to your television. No television? Even better. They suck a lot of electricity. Watch TV on your laptop instead.

You can use the money you save for so many alternative college activities. I guarantee you'll find some friends with cable, so you don't miss the big football game or absolutely-must-watch-because-it's-my-favorite TV show.

Sublet Your House or Apartment over the Summer

Most leases are for 12 months and many students go home for the summer. Paying for two or three months' rent when you're not even living there? That's gotta hurt!

Ease the pain by subletting your house or apartment (if your lease allows it). Be cautious, though. Not every renter is as conscientious as you. Try to sublet to someone who won't trash the place or throw crazy parties. Nothing is worse than moving in to start the new year, and finding a hole in the wall or mold in the sink because the person you let stay in your house didn't take care of it.

If you decide to sublet, go through the correct legal pro- ceedings and sign the appropriate documents. Always check with your landlord to see if it is a viable option.

Consider Becoming a Resident Advisor

Want to save thousands, even tens of thousands, on your college costs? Want to leave college with some great achievements to put on your resume? Want to get a jump-start on developing your leadership skills?

If you become a Resident Advisor (RA) (and this varies from school to school, so you need to inquire at yours), you will have room and board in the dorms for free. As you can imagine, this makes RA jobs hotly sought after.

Are you a good fit?

Being an RA is not for everyone. It takes a certain level of patience, self-esteem, and leadership skills to become a role model who'll be respected by the students in your dorm. This is not just a way to save money; it is a real job with real responsibilities.

RAs usually go through a rigorous training and must learn to balance their own needs with the needs of others. Being an RA can be fun, too, and you won't even look at it as a "job" after a while.

Travel

Keep Your Car at Home

Of course you love your car. Whether she's a sweet little Beetle with a flower on the dash or your mom's old minivan with coffee stains on the seats, cars are synonymous with independence and fun. But aside from tuition and rent, owning a car is the biggest cost in college. And unlike tuition and rent, it might be a non-necessity.

You might just find that having no car at school gives you even more independence!

Think about it. From gas and insurance to maintenance and mechanic visits, cars keep costing money. Unless your parents are picking up this tab, pass on bringing a car to college. You'll quickly meet many friends with cars and you can offer to split the gas with them.

If you can't find a friend with a car, check out the local public transportation: buses, trams, light rails, and occasionally taxis are all viable options.

However, I'd stay away from taxis as much as possible. They are the most expensive mode of transportation around town. Buses are often the cheapest. In some college towns, the buses are free for students, as long as you have your trusty college ID.

Check out ride sharing or one of those companies where car owners looking to make extra money will pick you up and drive you where you need to go.

A bike is a great way to get around town. If you haven't had one in years, you might just fall in love with biking. Remember to get a good, quality lock.

If all else fails, you can be that guy zipping around town on the scooter.

Carpool Home for the Holidays

Determined to get home for the holidays? That can be a hassle, especially if it's a long, boring, expensive drive. Search for someone who's going to the same place, or somewhere along the way, and carpool. Post a notice on your school's Facebook page, bulletin board, or just start asking around.

Carpooling gives you people to talk to, people to share the driving, and people to split the gas costs. The more people you take, the shorter the trip seems and the less broke you'll be when you get home.

Safety is the number one priority when picking a carpool buddy.

PLAN IN ADVANCE AND FLY CHEAPER

Flying can take as much strategizing as organizing a military campaign. Begin planning for flights to and from school at least three months out. This may guarantee the best rates and more flight time options. If it is a big travel weekend like Christmas or Valentine's Day, then plan even further in advance.

According to *USA Today*, the cheapest days to fly are Tuesdays, Wednesdays, and Saturdays. Take that into account when booking your tickets.

Southwest offers killer one-way ticket deals from certain hubs if you book online. These fill up quick, so don't wait! Also, check out prices on sites such as StudentUniverse.com before you book your flight.

Don't forget to sign up for frequent flyer miles, so after a few trips to and from school, you can earn a much-needed free flight.

Life Hacks

USE FREE SCHOOL PRINTERS

There's a reason printer ink is called "liquid gold." It's that expensive. I've paid more for my ink over the years than I paid for the printer itself. The budget-savvy option? Use the campus printers.

Not all campuses offer this service; if yours does, do a backflip. If yours doesn't, you'll have to get a bit more clever. Becoming a teaching or office assistant and many other jobs on campus may give you access to free printing. Also, certain departments may have free printing, so find out which ones do and print everything there.

Look around your college for local businesses offering discounted printing in bulk, or free printing for less than five pages.

If you prefer using your own printer, there are still ways to cut down on ink costs. Refilling and reusing your ink cartridges will be a huge saver for you. Check around online to find out if there are places in your town that refill ink. I'd be surprised if you don't find one.

My college babysitting job also helped me with printing costs. The family I worked for was kind enough to let me use their printer. People are rooting for you to be financially and academically successful. It never hurts to ask, "Can I use your printer for a ten-page assignment?"

(Please don't take advantage or use other people's printers without asking. When they go to print a document and find they are out of ink, you will likely be out of a job or out of a friendship.)

Employ the World's Greatest Problem Solver: Duct Tape

If you grew up with a handy dad who could fix anything good as new, you'll be missing him and his magic skills once you get to college.

Duct tape is the next best thing to Dad. (Don't tell him that.) Duct tape can fix just about anything. One friend had the bumper of her car attached with it (she found a color that was a perfect match) saving her an unimaginable fortune on body shop costs after her little ... ahem ... accident.

So don't throw things away just because they might be broken. Just wrap them up nice and cozy and secure in duct tape.

Think I'm kidding? According to ScienceChannel.com, "If duct tape is on Facebook, you should probably friend it now, before it gets so many friends it hires an intern to deny all your friend requests."

Duct tape, aka Duck tape, is priced just right for a starving student and it has numerous uses you might never have thought of. Look for it in the dollar store, of course! Get your "fix-it" on with some of these thrifty ideas:

- Found some free furniture with cracks or broken parts? Don't reject it—tape it! Perfect for old leather sofas and chairs. If you can't match the color, why not "reupholster" it and cover the entire cushion with duct tape? You do know it comes in cool colors and crazy patterns, don't you? Camo, anyone? How about leopard?
- Opened your door with too much force and it busted right through your wall? Duct tape to the rescue. You can even

paint right over it. I dare anyone to notice.

- Love your shoe collection but clutter at the bottom of your closet got you down? Make a shoe rack out of four stakes, a piece of cardboard and two rolls of duct tape.
- Fridge falling apart? Duct tape can hold together the handle or even the shelves on the door.
- Life falling apart? Not sure duct tape can help with that, but honestly, it's great for just about everything else. Don't be home without it.

Don't Buy Tech Without a Student ID

We love our tech, don't we? Technology is a common high school graduation present for students. Smartphones, iPads, and laptops fly off the shelves in preparation for students heading off to college. If you get everything you need as a gift, you're all set. But if you have to buy the things you'll need yourself, don't buy anything until you get that all-important school ID card.

Many companies offer large discounts to college students. Campus bookstores may have great prices for the technology you need as well. Why waste money? First find out what you need and compare the discounts at your bookstore before you buy anything.

CONSIGN UNUSED CLOTHES

Did you bring too much stuff with you, and find there's no room for it in the dorm? Did you go on some crazy precollege splurge and buy a bunch of stuff you'll never use? Have you gained the dreaded *freshman fifteen* and your clothes no longer fit?

Or are you simply foaming-at-the-mouth desperate for cash?

Selling old, never used, or barely used clothes, purses, and shoes is a great way to get a little extra cash in your pocket. Check out the consignment stores by your campus. Find the one that offers the best deal (they all have different terms) and take in all your unused, unloved, or unwanted treasures. A consignment shop only pays you if your stuff sells, so it's important to pay attention to the season. Scarves and sweaters won't sell in the summer, crop tops and cutoffs won't sell in the winter.

There are also resale shops, which pay cash for your stuff, right on the spot. You won't usually get as much as you would in a regular consignment shop, but you'll leave with cash in hand.

Consignment and retail shops will only buy what they think they can sell, so don't be offended if some of your stuff is rejected. Don't bring them anything shabby or worn, it definitely will be rejected.

Need new clothes? Consider consignment shops as well. They offer great deals to both buyer and seller.

BE BRAVE: LET BEAUTY STUDENTS CUT AND STYLE YOUR HAIR

Beauty school students touching your lovely, pampered locks? Do I hear you muttering *no way*? Hey, you're a student, so don't discriminate against other students! Although this is a great idea for guys, this tip is mostly addressed to you ladies.

Are you one of the many women who spend a small fortune dying and cutting your hair? You probably already know you won't be able to keep that up on your college budget, but do not despair.

Most beauty colleges provide super-inexpensive salon services so their students can get much needed experience. You will love the prices. Find a local beauty school and try it out. Start with a trim. If you click with a talented student, ask for her each time you go.

To dye or not to dye, that is the question.

You can dye your own hair or ask a friend to do it for you. If you've never done it before, it might take a few tries to get the exact shade you want. Read all instructions carefully before proceeding.

Bet you'll find lots of friends who dye their own hair who can advise and offer moral support. Clairol even has a hair dye hotline—1-800-CLAIROL!

If your auburn locks turn into a carrot top, don't panic. You won't be the first or the last. Adopt a calming new mantra: *It's only hair. It's only hair. It will grow back. It's only hair.*

DON'T PAY DOUBLE FOR MEDICAL INSURANCE

A re you covered under your parents' medical insurance? This is important to know. Some schools have health insurance programs that automatically cover their students. In some cases, if you don't *manually opt out* by submitting the required paperwork by a given deadline, you'll be stuck footing the bill for unnecessary insurance.

Ouch! That's enough to send you to the financial emergency room.

Review the cost and coverage of your current insurance thoroughly with your parents. They might have a better plan than your school does. However, you may even find that your campus health center is cheaper than going to an outside doctor through your parent's health insurance.

Find out in advance to ensure getting the best coverage and the best healthcare for the least cost.

Professional Matters

JOIN CLUBS

Clubs rock. When you join one (or two or three), you get to make insta-friends who share your interests, not to mention sharing the free pizza frequently served at meetings. Joining clubs is a great way to broaden your horizons with the limited amount of free time you have.

Look outside of your usual box when considering what clubs to join. College is the perfect time to explore things you were never interested in before, to hear new ideas, to hang out with all kinds of new and different people.

Who knows, that person next to you may become your best friend or boyfriend or business partner one day. You also may be happily surprised by the speakers who come on campus to talk to your club. Keep an open mind.

Apply for as Many Internships as Possible

I mentor college interns who are interested in getting into finance careers when they graduate and I'm extremely passionate about the value of internships. You can be sure my interns will have a leg-up on their non-intern competition when it comes time to get a job.

Strive to put one internship per year on your resume.

Here's why:

- Internships open eyes (and doors) to different careers or fields you might have overlooked.
- Internships give you a bird's-eye view of the real world.
- Internships give you the ability to rule out careers and jobs you don't want.
- Internships add experience, interest, and professionalism to a resume. Employers want to hire students who have taken initiative and have branched out.
- Make the time to squeeze in an internship, even if you only commit 5 hours per month. It's that important. Most colleges have multiple internships ready for students, and summer is the perfect time.

The value of internships cannot be overstated. Internships are vital to success in today's relentlessly competitive world. Not only do they show your initiative, they also provide experience and referrals that may, one day, seal the deal on a lucrative and fulfilling profession.

GET A JOB IF CASH FLOW IS TIGHT

If your allowance isn't cutting it, if you're running short ev- ery month, losing sleep at night, and piling on debt with your credit cards, you have two solutions.

First, find a way to cut back on your current spending. Second, find a part-time job to supplement your allowance. Tutoring is a great college job. Not only do you get paid, you also become an expert in that particular subject.

If possible, try to find a job in your major. Tell all your professors you're looking for a job. Keep reviewing job postings through your career center. Employers like me post jobs at local colleges and will take your school schedule into consideration.

Everything you do during your college years prepares you for the "real world." Who knows, this part-time job could end up being full time in the future.

START NETWORKING

This tip will not save you money, but I'd bet it will make you money somewhere down the line. Networking is one of the most important skills you can learn in school. I'm always stunned by how many adults can't or won't do it. But networking is really no different than socializing. In fact, it is socializing—but in a purely professional way.

Mastering networking gives you the self-confidence and the social skills and the contacts to achieve success. Remember, it's just as much about who you know as what you know … and it always will be.

I've seen some really smart people fall far short of their potential because they were book smart, they were technology smart, but they had no communication skills. They didn't know how to engage professionally with others. They had no sense of appropriate behavior. Sad but true.

And believe it or not, that's what employers in the country are looking for today—people with what are called "soft skills:" communication skills, leadership skills, listening skills, people skills.

Use these four years to practice your social skills; they are more important than you think.

If you are not on LinkedIn, get on it today. This powerful social site is all about professional networking. It lets you connect with your parents' friends, your professors, and potential employers that speak on campus—even business leaders or professionals in your field whom you admire.

Connect with everyone you meet on LinkedIn.

The savvy professional networker who is looking out for his or her future does follow up. Input potential business contacts into a file. Add reminders to check in with your contacts quarterly. You never know when you'll drop someone a line (via email — not text) to say hi, and they'll tell you about a great job that might be perfect for you.

ALWAYS PAY IT FORWARD

Paying it forward merely means doing something nice for someone else without them ever asking. The classic example is going through a toll booth and paying for the guy behind you as well.

Why on earth would you want to do that? For starters, paying it forward is a very positive and proactive state of mind. It creates the habit of doing nice things for other people without expecting anything in return, showing that you are kind and thoughtful and selfless. Employers love those kinds of people and will go out of their way to hire them. Pay-it-forwarders are the kind of people everyone wants to hang out with and work with.

Is that you? I'm not saying you have to spend all your money on strangers, not at all.

Examples of paying it forward:

- If you see a job opportunity for a friend, reach out to them and help make the connection.
- Share old books or furniture with other students who need them.
- Help others network who might not be as good at it as you are.
- Volunteer to help someone move.
- Bring a friend home for the weekend to do laundry or enjoy Mom's home-cooked meal.

KEEP YOUR WILD SIDE OFF SOCIAL MEDIA

Take a walk on the wild side if you must. That's part of what college is about for many kids. But … and this is a *big but*— please don't tweet about it. Or selfie it. Or Insta- gram it. Get it?

Go through your Social Media sites and take off all the inappropriate pictures you wouldn't want your future employer to see. And trust me, they *will* look.

Delete all those wild party pictures. All those four-letter- word-filled posts. Any naked pictures. Any thing that hints of violence, racism, sexism, and any other inappropriate ism. Delete, delete, delete. Get rid of any phone apps that tempt you to post inappropriate pictures or messages during parties, thus leaving you to post only when you're in front of your computer in a more serious and rational state of mind.

You've heard of twunking? Yep, that stands for tweeting drunk. Don't. It will come back to haunt you.

Every picture or status update you post on social media is PUBLIC. It can easily be seen by the people around you and your future employers. Would your grandma approve of your post?

Speaking as an employer, I check social media sites to de- termine if I want to hire someone. Inappropriate posts could end up costing you the best job opportunity of your life.

One last thing. If you go on an interview, never say anything negative about the interview, the interviewer, or the company on social media. This type of ignorance has cost many people plum jobs in today's transparent age.

Don't Shy Away from Opportunities

Colleges work hard to bring the best recruiters and other job opportunities on campus. They want you to be successful when you graduate. Don't pass up these amazing op-portunities by sitting in your dorm room or going to a party when you could be … drumroll … networking!

Attend every career fair or dinner or talk hosted by pro-fessors from your major. Get out of your comfort box and your room by attending events and going out of your way to introduce yourself to students or professors you haven't met yet. Listen to their innovative ideas; you never know who will be the next Bill Gates.

Get to know people. Talk to them about their ideas. Maybe they'll want your help with one of their projects or startups. Talk to your professors and your friends' parents as well. This is all part of mastering those social skills we talked about earlier.

Opportunities will come knocking at your door; however, they generally will not come knocking at your dorm room door. Get out, get connecting, and you'll build the courage you need to take advantage of great opportunities when they come your way.

Attend professional events in a suit or other business attire and be well-groomed. No scraggly weeks' worth of unshaved beard. No sweats. No workout clothes, no matter how stylish they may look. No exceptions.

See my tip on "Dress for Success."

MAKE A BUSINESS CARD

But you don't have a business? No matter. Here's the deal on the ubiquitous business card. At career fairs and alumni weekends, employers receive thousands of resumes from prospective students vying for internships or jobs. Make yourself stand out! Have a business card and make it easy for them to remember you. Not only does it show that you took the time and effort to make one, it will go into their wallet instead of into a pile on their desk.

Your business card does not need to be a design masterpiece. However, it does need to be visually appealing to your future employer. A few basic tips to get you on the right track:

- Font needs to be easy to read and at least size 11. Nothing too fancy.
- Use quality printing with no risk of ink smearing. White or beige paper are always a good choice.
- Include all your necessary contact information. See example below.

You can design and order your business cards online. Look around and you'll find great deals, or you can make one at a paper supply store or copy store such as Kinko's or FedEx.

Example:

```
┌─────────────────────────────┐
│            Name             │
│           Address           │
│                             │
│        Phone Number         │
│            Email            │
└─────────────────────────────┘
```

DRESS FOR SUCCESS

I f you want to be taken as a serious, hirable professional, please wear a suit or other professional attire to every event that entails competition. This includes interviews, career fairs, and meetings to view potential rental properties. People are more willing to offer opportunities to those who look the part.

If you have no idea what is appropriate, err on the side of conservative. If you have no suit, get thee to the consignment shop post haste. You only need one good, well-pressed, well-fitting suit in college. No one will mind if you wear it more than once.

I am shocked to see students in flip-flops and shorts at events where they're interacting with potential employers. Sorry, I wouldn't hire you if you look like you just rolled out of bed. That does not show any effort, respect, or professionalism.

Why would I assume you would do a professional job or represent my company in the way I'd like it to be represent- ed? Guaranteed, I am not the only business owner who feels this way, even in the laid-back twenty-first century.

Hopefully, your hair will look professional (time to hit the beauty school), nails done (no paint chips), and a fresh scent is always nice. Have one suit clean and ready to be worn at all times. Sure, you may be overdressed at some events, but who cares? Your professors are watching; they *will* notice if you're dressed professionally and acting professionally at these events. A great reference from a professor can seal the deal on the job you really want sometime in the future.

Remember, dressing formally and looking crisp is an important first step. When it comes to opportunities, you only get one chance to make a great first impression.

WORK HARD, PLAY HARD

This is the motto I've based my whole life on. College life is no different. Work hard on your studies; find time to release some steam by playing just as hard.

Playing hard can be your workout regime, time with your friends, hobbies, listening to music, going home to see family/friends, whatever brings a smile to your face and rests your soul. Take the time to find this work/play balance and clearly identify what gives you peace and satisfaction at the end of each day.

College is not easy. Unless you're a genius, you'll probably have to push yourself hard to get the grades you desire. But life is also not easy. The balancing act of working hard and then rewarding yourself by playing hard will be part of your everyday life. If you adopt my motto, you will achieve. You'll never be bored. You'll give yourself and your life your all. And that's a great feeling.

ALWAYS WRITE THANK-YOU NOTES

Hand-written thank-you notes have become almost archaic in today's society. Have you ever seen one? Fewer and fewer people send snail mail thank-you cards for gifts. Instead, they call or send an email. This is fine much of the time.

But you'll really stand out as a class act if you send the old-fashioned, still-relevant thank-you note. It's the personal touch and the extra effort that make the difference. Sending an email is just not the same.

(Please don't even consider a thank-you text. I gag to think of it.)

A thank-you note sent to a potential new employer after an interview, thanking them for the opportunity, can make a big difference. Especially to those employers who are looking for people with good communication and people skills. Your hand-written thank-you note shows you have what they are looking for.

Send one to that professor who went out of his way to open a door for you with a potential employer. Again, a writ- ten thank-you shows you care enough to take the time to write a note and will leave a lasting, good impression—very valuable if you ever need that professor's help again.

Writing a thank-you note takes 60 seconds. What excuse could you find not to do this? To save money, don't buy single cards. Buy a box of cards or a box of nice-looking stationary. Many times a whole box of cards will cost about the same as one individual card. You can buy bulk boxes of generic cards at your local stores like Target or Walmart or maybe even your dollar store. Remember, it's what you write in the card that counts. Include your business card in every note.

DON'T CHANGE AFTER GRADUATION

The biggest mistake students make after graduating and getting a job? Splurging! They immediately forget the whole *living life frugally* thing and go on a spending binge, never sign up for any investment or retirement plans, or worse, get into mega-credit-card debt.

Fight the urge to splurge. Okay, one paycheck. I don't want you to live like a Scrooge.

But the more money you save when you're young, the more you will thank yourself when you are older and have a family. Remember, saving is sexy. Saving is smart. Saving is the way to freedom. Keep these same money-managing practices after graduation and you will always stay afloat.

Welcome to the
Real World

Closing Thoughts ...

Congratulations! You've graduated college—no small feat—and you are now entering a different chapter in your life, what I like to call the "real world." New colleagues, new challenges, complete independence, and an incredible amount of personal responsibility await you.

Many students are afraid to leave their college cocoon and step out alone. If that's how you feel, honest, you're not alone. If you're questioning your ability to achieve success, first, take a deep breath. Okay, one more. I can tell you many things that will help.

This is your time to start making money and focusing on your contributions to the world. Energy and passion for life may be pouring out of every pore in your body. Hopefully, you get up every morning and think, "Let's do this!"

Embrace that spirit and run with it.

Statistically speaking, it's unlikely you'll get your dream job right out of college. No problem! Most new grads move around a fair bit until they find their niche. It doesn't mean there's anything wrong with you or your education or the economy. Your first job will be a stepping stone to the next. That's just how it works.

Which is great, really, because you want to get some experience under your belt before you tackle your dream job. No matter how hard you studied, no matter what you learned, a "real" job is going to be very different.

Let's review how to handle your finances. Solid guidelines on how to handle your money, whether it's pitiful pennies or buckets of gold, will go a long way to building your confidence the first few months.

The temptation to splurge will be all around you, 24/7, once you've landed your new job. Don't do it! Step awaaaay from that cash register.

Initially, finances in the adult world will not be much different than when you were in college. You might be in awe of your paycheck and ecstatic to have money coming in regularly. So learn to balance the funds coming in so they don't go out too fast.

Be smart with your money.

Visualize various buckets and plan to fill them each to overflowing. Doesn't that sound awesome? Consider one bucket for retirement (yes, the R word again), one for emergency reserves (emergencies happen), one to pay down debt (which you have minimized as much as possible by being thrifty during college), and one for day-to-day expenses. Including some fun!

These seven tips will get you on the right track, regardless of your salary.

- Create a new budget. You know how to make one that works for you. You know how to stay on it. Get used to the idea that until you make your gazillions, you will always need a budget. Remember, budgets are sexy. Budgets are cool. Budgets breed confidence and self-respect. Which would you rather have: self-respect? Or a new pair of shoes you'll feel bad about every time you wear them because you can't make rent?

- Okay, back to business. It's crucial to have a clear breakdown of the amount of money that is coming in and going out each month. Identify your categories and allocate a budget to each one of those areas.

- Save 20% of your income in a retirement plan. We've talked about this a few times already. I know you want to take the money you're earning and just let loose ... just have some fun ... buy all the things you want ... go on great vacations with your peeps. I get it. I do.

- Retirement seems like an eternity away at this point in your life. But please don't wait. Don't think, "Geez, I just graduated. Retirement is forty years off at least. I've got plenty of time." Be savvier than that. I've seen too many people who waited way too long to start saving for retirement. Once you get into the 20% hab- it, you'll never miss that money.

- Many employers offer a retirement plan and possibly will match a percentage of your contribution. Read the plan description for all details. These plans make it convenient to save because the money is deducted directly from your paycheck. It's painless!

- Create an emergency fund totaling six months of living expenses. This won't happen overnight. It may take years to create. Open a *separate savings account* for your emergency reserves. Having this money will be a lifesaver if you lose your job and can't immediately find a new one, or you decide to move to a new city to look for work, or your car drops dead and cannot be resuscitated, or any other type of emergency occurs.

- Pay off all debt as soon as you can. Think ball and chain weighing you down. No debt is good debt, so keep a laser focus on debt destruction. Don't just pay the minimum balances—you'll never pay it off that way. Add additional funds to the principal.

- Complete"The *Everything* Binder."(Details in the back of the book.) If something happens to you, your family will have all your financial, estate, and personal affairs organized in one location. Completing this binder will give you the peace of mind that if anything happens to you, death or disability, everything is documented for your loved ones.

- Find a fee-based financial planner and build a financial plan. Have clear goals in place, so you never question your   financial position. Update this financial plan once a year to evaluate your progress.
- If you are in a committed relationship, disclose your finances and worries surrounding money or saving or the stock market. Don't hide anything. I have seen unwillingness to be open about money sink many a relationship. Instead, just talk to your partner about your opinions of money, how you were raised around money, and your spending habits when you're happy or depressed. Lay it all on the line, because money is one of the major stressors in marriages and you want to always have open communication with your partner.

Growing into adulthood is not that hard. Billions of people have done it. The question is how successfully do you want to do it? And how do you define success?

I'm excited and delighted for you as you head out to your new life, precious and hard-won diploma in hand. I wish you all the success in the world, in whatever forms matter to *you*.

APPENDIX A

Money Coming In	
	Amount ($)
Job Income	$
Financial Aid	$
Parental Allowance	$
Student Loans	$
Total	$
Money Going Out	
	Amount ($)
Rent	$
Electricity	$
Water	$
Trash	$
Groceries/Dining Out	$
Cable/Internet/Phone	$
Auto Expenses	$
Laundry	$
Haircuts	$
Clothing	$
Toiletries	$
Social Expenses	$
Miscellaneous	$
Total	$

Emergency Reserve Fund

(Save monthly for this reserve.)	
	Amount ($)
Beginning Balance	$
Monthly Additions	-
January	$
February	$
March	$
April	$
May	$
June	$
July	$
August	$
September	$
October	$
November	$
December	$
Total	$

APPENDIX B

Credit Card Payoff Tracker

Name of Card			
Month	January	February	March
Balance	$_____	$_____	$_____
Annual percentage rate (APR)	_____%	_____%	_____%
Minimum Payment	$_____	$_____	$_____
Additional Principal	$_____	$_____	$_____
Number of Months to Payoff			

Sources

1   Stephanie Weers, "5 Reasons to Stop Wearing Sweatpants to
    Class," *USA Today*, October 29, 2012, http://college.usato-
    day.com/2012/10/29/5-reasons-to- stop-wearing-sweatpants-
    to-class/

2   Rick Seaney, "Airfare Expert: The Three Cheapest Days to
    Fly," *USA Today*, August 26, 2014,
    http://www.usatoday.com/story/travel/columnist/se-
    aney/2014/08/26/cheap-airfare-plane-ticket/14573015/

3   "Top 10 Uses for Duct Tape," Science Channel,
    http://www.sciencechannel.com/science-technology/ 10-
    uses-for-duct-tape.htm

ACKNOWLEDGMENTS

I am so lucky to have an amazing team to help launch this book. Thanks to Ryan Dennehy for researching every tip and reminding me how much fun college is, despite how poor you might feel. To Catherine Hall and Kimberly Miller, thank you for your valuable input. Thank you to my editing team, Leslie Miller and Margaret Koscho, who always make my sentences look so beautiful.

Endless thanks to Saint Mary's College, Moraga California, for giving me the funds to attend your school and opening countless doors for me. To my friends at the *Wall Street Journal*, who motivated me to write this book, because you continually asked me to write on college savings ideas on the Expert Panel.

And to my loving family, Jared, Lauren, and Ella. I am blessed to have you in my life every day.

Lauren and Ella, remember these tips when you go off to college. Mom loves you!

OTHER BOOKS BY MICHELLE

Stocks, Bonds & Soccer Moms: 7 Steps to a Balanced Life

Women these days have been raised to believe they can *have it all*. And they can—if they can learn to find balance, both inner and outer.

Michelle Perry Higgins had a fabulous marriage, a healthy child, a mega-powered career, and enough stress and imbal- ance to almost ruin everything.

In this Amazon best-seller, Michelle reveals the seven steps she took to bring herself and her life back into balance.

Each chapter in the book reveals one of the steps to balance in detail, along with practical tips and suggestions, and clear, heart-felt advice. The results:

A happier, healthier, more confident you!

Buy Now: www.MichellePerryHiggins.com

The Everything Binder Book:
Financial, Estate, and Personal Affairs Organizer

The Everything Binder is the essential all-in-one storage system for all your most important information, including:

Pre & Post-Death Checklists	*Medical History*
Important Contacts	*Insurance*
Document Originals & Copies	*Debt*
Personal Property	*Funeral Arrangements*
Retirement & Investments	*Pet Information*
Income & Cash Equivalents	*And much more!*

The Everything Binder Book is an easy-to-use organization system. If an accident, illness, or death occurs, your family or trusted friends will turn to this helpful tool for answers.

Buy Now: www.MichellePerryHiggins.com

ABOUT THE AUTHOR

As a financial planner and principal of California Financial Advisors in San Ramon, California, Michelle Perry Higgins specializes in wealth management. Since 1996 she has built a successful practice advising executive professionals into retirement, and her passion for finance has helped hundreds of individuals better understand the process of investing and fiscal planning.

Ms. Higgins was ranked in the Top 50 Women-Owned RIAs in 2013, Top 25 Women RIAs in 2012 and 2014, and Top 40 Under 40 by WealthManagement.com. Also, she was awarded the 2012, 2013, and 2014 Five Star Wealth Manager Award, *Diablo Magazine*. She has appeared on CNBC and CBS, quoted in Yahoo! *Finance, MSN Money, Los Angeles Times*, Examiner.com and is a *Wall Street Journal* Expert Panelist. Ms. Higgins is a frequent public speaker on retirement planning, investments, wealth management, college education funding, estate planning, and insurance. In addition, she has published two books: *The Everything Binder: Financial, Estate, and Personal Affairs Organizer* and *Stocks, Bonds & Soccer Moms: 7 Steps to a Balanced Life.*

Ms. Higgins graduated from Saint Mary's College with a concentration in business administration and economics. Currently, she is on the Saint Mary's College Women's Leadership Council as it is her passion to give back by mentoring young women and helping to raise scholarship funds.

Ms. Higgins enjoys spending time with her husband and their two daughters.

ABOOKS

ALIVE Book Publishing and ALIVE Publishing Group
are imprints of Advanced Publishing LLC,
3200 A Danville Blvd., Suite 204, Alamo, California 94507

Telephone: 925.837.7303
alivebookpublishing.com

www.ingramcontent.com/pod-product-compliance
Lightning Source LLC
Chambersburg PA
CBHW022057210326
41519CB00054B/558